PRESIDENT LINCOLN'S THIRD LARGEST CITY

BROOKLYN AND THE CIVIL WAR

BY
E. A. (BUD) LIVINGSTON

CONTENTS

I could say that I almost gave up on this entire project. This, however, would be untrue. I did give up.

And while discussing the difficulties of finding information about Civil War Brooklyn I related my tale to Marie Reno and Steve Jaffe, members of the Civil War Round Table of New York. They talked me into working at the task in a different manner. Without their encouragement I never would have produced this book.

Both Marie and Judy Hallock helped enormously in reading, editing, and making suggestions as how to better the manuscript, and Dr. Frank Merli of the history department of Queens College is mostly responsible for whatever decent writing you will find here.

Burt and Dana Levine allowed me to use their Apple computer for my master's degree and this book is just an outgrowth of that paper. Others who helped in major or minor ways were Pat Falci, Roslyn Roth, Malcolm and Cherokee Stock, Terry Hunt, Clare Lamers, (the Brooklyn Historical Society's quintessential librarian), my sister Shari, my daughter Julie, her husband, Peter Gordon, (my computer expert who continually got me out of tangled messes on my word processor), my son Daniel and his wife, Donna, Pat and Dick Merrill, Ari and Olive Hoogenboom, Paul Nergelovic of the West Point library, James O. Hall, Edith Bartley of the Plymouth Church, Dr. Edwin Redkey, Dr. William Seraille, Dr. Robert Swan, Ben Maryniak, Joe Geden, Lex Paradis, John Willetts, the Honorable Frank Raymond, Jack Mulloy, Nancy Moore and Ron Nelson. Nancy and Ron, thousands of miles away, gave me indescribable encouragement. Ernie and Hedwig Ries translated ante-bellum German church records and Arthur Konop, the archivist at Saint Francis College taught me that all of Brooklyn was Kings County but all of Kings County was not Brooklyn. Harvey Appelbaum created that wonderful cover and Fred Halla, of the Brooklyn Heights <u>Weekly Record</u>, was kind enough to be the first to publish my work for the general public.

And a very special thanks goes to Robert Creamer, one of the country's foremost sports writers. He mentioned me in his book <u>Baseball in '41</u> and it would be churlish of me not to mention him here.

GEOGRAPHY

Brooklyn, New York: land area eighty-one square miles; located at seventy-three degrees fifty-eight minutes west longitude and forty degrees forty minutes north latitude; highest elevation: Greenwood Cemetery, two hundred sixteen feet; lowest elevation: sea level; widest point; nine and one half miles between the East River and the Queens County border; greatest length: eleven and one half miles from Greenpoint in the north to Coney Island in the south. Approximately sixty-five miles of natural shoreline. Part of the Atlantic Coastal Plain, a geological region which stretches from north of New York City to Florida; its features include a rolling plain of the Pleistocene Age, a terminal moraine, and a broad outwash plain created by a retreating glacier 13,000 years ago.[1]

---

[1] Brooklyn Almanac, edited by Margaret Lattimer(Brooklyn, 1984), pp. 10, 11.

INTRODUCTION

On the very first day of the year 1898, the city of Brooklyn ceased to exist.[1]

As its independent status ended it became just another section of its giant neighbor, New York. And yet the former city still had enough special characteristics left to have a major league baseball team - the Brooklyn Dodgers[2] - and a world - famous accent, no mean feats. Despite its subsumption it remained in many ways a separate entity. Many natives respond "Brooklyn" and not "New York" when asked about their origins.

During its heyday the city enjoyed a special reputation. On the eve of the Civil War Brooklyn's population exceeded that of every other American city except Philadelphia and New York,[3] and its waterfront facilities transshipped most of America's western grain exports. While the Brooklyn Navy Yard employed over five thousand workers daily, another shipyard, the Continental Iron Works, built a unique vessel that altered naval warfare forever. Adopted son Walt Whitman became one of America's best known and most controversial poets, and George W. Goethals, future builder of the Panama Canal, attended public school near his home in Brooklyn Heights. Elias P. Howe, Jr. sold sewing machines from his house, having obtained the first American patent on that invention, and Peter Cooper, one day to lend his name to Cooper Union, ran a glue factory near the Maspeth border. German immigrant Samuel Liebmann made lager beer in a factory near Bushwick Avenue and called his product Rheingold, while two of the country's major pharmaceutical companies, Squibb and Pfizer both begun in Brooklyn, thrived during the Civil War. Local manufacturers made an incredible variety of products ranging from macaroni to oil cloth, including the first American-made, commercially produced chinaware. The Greenpoint neighborhood provided work for thirty-five per cent of its working population in the shipbuilding trade, and the city's Dime Savings Bank may have started the bank-by-mail system by dealing with peripatetic soldiers.

The city's major theatre featured leading performers of the day, including John Wilkes Booth, who played there twice in 1863. Brooklyn's most famous house of worship, the Plymouth Church, led by the country's most controversial clergyman, Henry Ward Beecher, gained the attention of presidential candidate Abraham Lincoln, when he visited there in 1860. Brooklyn sported four well known and excellent base ball [4] teams, one of which made the very first base ball tour, playing in Western New York State, Philadelphia and Baltimore, giving our future national pastime its greatest boost ever .

These aforementioned "surprises" form a foundation for Brooklyn's claim to greatness. It might have been famous but for one insuperable impediment: its proximity to New York City.

[1] New York Times, January 1, 1898.
   Brooklyn became a city in 1834.
[2] Major league baseball teams took the names of various cities and states. No team, however, with the exception of the Brooklyn Dodgers, was ever named after only a section of a city.
[3] Rosen, Elliot A., The Growth of the American City 1839-1860, doctoral dissertation, New York University, 1953, p. 344.
[4] 1860 spelling

GENERAL DESCRIPTION

Swelled by the arrival of Irish and German immigrants and a steady flow of middle-class families from overcrowded Manhattan, Brooklyn's ever-increasing population placed it seventh among American cities in 1854. On January 1, 1855, however, with the annexation of the city of Williamsburgh (fifty thousand) and the town of Bushwick (seven thousand), Brooklyn now claimed more than two hundred seventy-nine thousand residents, making it the third largest city in the United States.[1] The newcomers had so many different religious affiliations that Brooklyn became known as the "City of Churches." One house of worship in particular, Henry Ward Beecher's Plymouth Church, would gain national fame.[2]

Brooklyn's name, an Anglicized version of Breuckelen, one of the original towns of Kings County,[3] may have been derived from a place near Utrecht, Holland, although it also could have merely been a mispronunciation of "broken land" or "brook land." The original six towns, one English (Gravesend), and the others Dutch (Flatbush, Flatlands, New Utrecht, Breuckelen and Bushwick) merged into Kings County in 1683 and adopted the Dutch motto "Een draght maakt maght (unity makes strength).[4]

By 1860 Brooklyn had become one of America's great manufacturing centers and claimed a complex and varied industrial base. Its factories wended their way along the shoreline from Red Hook in the south to Williamsburg [5] and Greenpoint along the East River, and Newtown Creek in the north. Part of Brooklyn's growth resulted from its proximity to the congested metropolis of New York, the country's largest city, whose heavily concentrated industrial and commercial districts could no longer handle further growth. Manufacturers, forced to cram their operations into crowded downtown loft buildings, sometimes in several locations, saw great potential in the unlimited space of north Brooklyn. Here, in a single location, factories could convert raw materials and ship finished goods quickly and inexpensively. And manufacturers could still administer their business from New York, only a five-minute, two-cent ferry ride across the East River.[6]

Despite the industrialized activities of shipyards, distilleries, glass works, and casting furnaces, much of Brooklyn remained bucolic. Newspapers often ran ads for lost cows, along with news of cattle rustling in the hamlet of Bedford. Coming in from Flatbush, visitors found mostly open space until they reached the Bull's Head Tavern on Brooklyn's border. Then they saw houses, few and scattered; first shacks, then some farmhouses, and finally large elegant homes with huge front lawns.[7]

Except for the Navy Yard area, Brooklyn seemed a quiet place where, below the Heights, businesssmen, clerks, and mechanics built rows of small, square houses on lots of twenty-five by one hundred; modest homes at moderate cost. The city's nocturnal population outnumbered its daytime residents by about thirty thousand, as approximately ten per cent of its business people ferried to Manhattan in the morning and returned at night. This made Brooklyn one of New York's first bedroom communities.[8]

New York's metropolitan region expanded greatly soon after Robert Fulton's steam ferry <u>Nassau</u>, built in the

Brooklyn Navy Yard, began to ply the East River waters in 1816.[9] By 1860 thousands of immigrants, similar in origin to those in New York, crossed the river to Brooklyn and stayed, raising the city's foreign-born population to thirty-seven per cent, some one hundred four thousand people. Of these, fifty-four per cent came from Ireland, twenty-five per cent from the German states,[10] seventeen per cent from Great Britain, and the balance from France, Canada, and other places. The black population of forty-nine hundred remained constant throughout the Civil War.[11]

Of New York natives who left Manhattan, the largest number settled in Brooklyn, and by 1865 more than three hundred thousand people resided in Kings County. By comparison, Queens County (the towns of Flushing, Jamaica and Newtown) had thirty thousand, Richmond County (Staten Island) had twenty thousand, and New York County (Manhattan) eight hundred thirty-one thousand. Westchester County (including the Bronx) had ninety-nine thousand.[12]

An educational center, Brooklyn had many fine medical institutions, including the Long Island College Hospital, one of the first to use the European method of teaching.[13] The city's many public and private schools included the Polytechnic Institute on Livingston Street for young men and the Packer Collegiate Institute on Montague Street for young women. The public school system also produced a solid education as attested to by George W. Goethals, who attended Public School number 15 near his State Street home during the Civil War.[14]

Montague Street's Academy of Music played an important role in Brooklyn's social life as the community used it for amateur theatricals, charity balls, and political and temperance meetings. But the Academy's main purpose, to present the best contemporary performers and works, succeeded admirably as Edwin Forrest, Laura Keene, John McCullough, Edwin Booth, and his brother, John Wilkes Booth, among many others, all acted on its stage.[15]

The city, vibrant and productive, had many good things going for it. To many people, however, it was still only an adjunct of New York. Brooklyn constantly strove to prove otherwise.

[1] Syrett, Harold, The City of Brooklyn 1865-1898 A Political History(New York, 1944), pp.12,13
Rosenwaike, Ira, Population History of New York City(Syracuse, 1972), p.50.
The History of the City of Brooklyn, edited by Henry R. Stiles, Brooklyn, 1867-1870, 3 vol., vol.2, p.420.

[2] The Great Divine, Henry Ward Beecher, pamphlet, Brooklyn Historical Society, 1986, (hereafter B.H.S.)
The City of Brooklyn, A Political History, p.20.

[3] In this work all of Kings County shall be considered Brooklyn, even though in 1861 the rural towns of Flatbush, Flatlands, New Utrecht, Gravesend and New Lots were not part of the city. Also, since the city of New York and the state of New York share the same name, any reference to "New York," or "Manhattan," will be to the city; references to the state will be indicated as "New York State."

[4] Brooklyn Almanac, p.20,21.
Armbruster, Eugene, Brujkleen Colonie 1638-1918,

pamphlet, 1918, New York Historical Society, (hereafter N.Y.H.S.).

[5] The final "h" was dropped after consolidation.

[6] Factories, Foundries and Refineries, edited by Joshua Brown and David Ment, pamphlet, B.H.S., pp. 5-7.

[7] Brooklyn City News, March 22, 1862.
New York Times, October 2, 1861.
Brooklyn, Old and New, pamphlet, Dime Savings Bank of Brooklyn Archives, 1927, Herman Eberhard, archivist.

[8] The City of Brooklyn, A Political History, p.11.
Factories, Foundries and Refineries, p.9.
Kaplan, Justin, Walt Whitman, A Life(New York, 1980), pp.71.

[9] Wolfe, Gerard R., New York, A Guide to the Metropolis (New York, 1975), p.325.
Growing Up In Brooklyn, Martha McGowan, pamphlet, Brooklyn Union Gas Company, 1983, p.8,.

[10] The modern country of Germany did not exist until 1871.

[11] Population History of New York City, pp.50,55,64.
Growing Up in Brooklyn, p.8.

[12] Ibid.,pp.51,64.

[13] American medical school training was almost always limited to lectures only. The European method included visits to patients. Main Artery, silver centennial issue of the Long Island College Hospital newsletter, p.2.

[14] Main Artery.
Miller's New York As It Is, pp. 99,100,111.
Bishop, Joseph, and Bishop, Farnham, George Goethals, Genius of the Panama Canal(New York,1930), p.27.

[15] Growing Up In Brooklyn, p.9.
Brooklyn Academy of Music, special brochure.

THE PEOPLE

The Dutch elite of Brooklyn had family lines that went back to the 1600's. Their ancestors had been rewarded with tracts of land in Breuckelen, Flatbush, Flatlands or New Utrecht for their roles in the social and political intrigues of that day. This elite practiced endogamy, marrying within their class, as Cortelyous married Van Pelts and Suydams married Vorheeses. The list of Brooklyn's well-to-do Dutch families reads like a street directory: Rapelye, Boerum, Gerritsen, Lefferts, Schenck, Martense, Cortelyou, Van Sinderen, Van Nostrand, Remsen, and Schermerhorn. The second largest group of "old" Brooklyn had roots in New England, but other wealthy and influential families had different backgrounds, including the Zabriskies of Prussia, the Fleets and Halseys of England, the Debevoises of France, the Emburys of Germany and the Murphys of Ireland.[1]

Not all of Brooklyn's families, however, came from such well established backgrounds. Although mostly a city of middle-class people, Brooklyn's population represented all socio-economic groups. Many of its poor, especially recent Irish and German immigrants, lived in dingy, crowded tenements or in flimsy shacks, eking out a living by menial labor.[2]

Brooklyn's growth mimicked that of its giant neighbor across the river, and any increase in the number of immigrants to the former generally meant corresponding increases in the latter. This became especially true around 1830 when Manhattan became so congested that building could not keep pace with the arrival of newcomers.[3]

THE IRISH

The largest immigrant group came from the Emerald Isle. More than fifty thousand Irish, fleeing the Great Potato Famine, migrated to New York in 1846, and many crossed the East River to settle in Brooklyn. Most were farmers, although passenger lists show many mechanics and clerks among them. The entrenched Protestant elite viewed them with disdain as they had little education, less money, and a religion considered not only un-American, but one dominated by a foreign ruler. With values and beliefs so different, and a speech pattern many found painful to the ear, they might just spread what the nativist Know-Nothing Party called the "Roman Menace," a danger not only to Brooklyn but to the country at large. They also seemed to take easily to drink, song, and dance, and this too proved distasteful to the stolid Kings County aristocracy. Their apparent disrespect for the law, possibly a result of their unpleasant experience with the English penal system, gave the "Paddies" a status in the New York/Brooklyn area close to that of the Negroes in the south. Many considered them the crime problem of the north.[4]

The Gaelic influx created an Irish ghetto in Brooklyn's Western District, the fifth ward. This Irishtown ran from Concord Street in the south to the East River on the north, and from Bridge Street on the west to Little and Hudson streets on the east. The Eastern District's Irish lived near Metropolitan, Meeker, Bushwick and Union Avenues.[5]

Many immigrants, like Cornelius Rea Agnew, founder of the Brooklyn Eye and Ear Hospital, furrier Cornelius Heeney, attorney Henry C. Murphy, and Thomas Kinsella, editor of the Brooklyn <u>Eagle</u>, gained success, but all too many Irish fared poorly in the big city. Serious problems arose in the transition from farm to urban life. In place of clean fresh air the new Americans now lived in the stench of malodorous slums where unsanitary conditions promoted cholera and tuberculosis. The easy access to liquor in the local taverns served as an escape for some, and drunkenness became common. Many young girls became prostitutes in order to provide food and clothing for large families, some plying their trade along Fulton Street, and Irish boys all too often became petty thieves.[6] In 1859, fifty-five per cent of males arrested in the New York area were transplanted Irishmen. In New York State, of the publicly supported paupers, eighty-six per cent were foreign-born and of this group fifty-three per cent were Irish immigrants.[7] Typhoid, consumption, accidents, and childbirth accounted for the majority of deaths recorded in the fifth ward, and children under the age of six accounted for sixty-four per cent of the deaths recorded there in 1865.[8]

Irish women found work as servants or cooks[9] and the men, called "spalpeens" in the old country, provided cheap day labor for the construction trade. They dug the Gowanus Canal and laid track for the horsecar lines that employed them later as drivers or conductors. Hard pressed to eke out a living in ante-bellum Brooklyn, they had no sympathy for black slaves in the south, or free Negroes anywhere, and they feared that a flood of freedmen would threaten their low paid jobs. When the Civil War became a war to free the slaves, the Irish objected. Their economic problems should be addressed first, they believed, prior to fighting a war that they perceived as being waged to benefit black slaves whose lives quite often seemed far easier than their own.[10]

In 1860, presidential candidate Stephen Douglas received strong support in every northern city with a sizable Gaelic population. Even after his death in 1861 the Irish remembered him in a popular enlistment poem:

> To the tenets of Douglas we tenderly cling
> Warm hearts to the cause of our country we bring
> To the flag we are pledged all its foes we abhor
> And we ain't for the nigger but we are for the war.[11]

Their many problems notwithstanding, when the Civil War began the Irish rushed to the colors, prompting the Standard to comment that "fighting is an Irishman's trade." And fight they did. For a variety of reasons, some economic, some patriotic, they volunteered their services in droves. Some estimates claimed that more than fifty thousand of New York State's three hundred thirty-eight thousand soldiers had come from Ireland, and no less than thirty-eight Union regiments had the word "Irish" in their names. Opinion varied, but many believed that the Irish had become the nonpareil of Union soldiers.[12]

An Irish melody, "Eibhleen a Ruin" (Treasure of My Heart), given lyrics in the eighteenth century, became known popularly as "Robin Adair." Its American version served as a recruiting song called "Flag of the Free."

> Could we desert you now
> Flag of the Free;
> When we a solemn vow,
> Flag of the Free,
> You to all harm to save

Made when we crossed the wave
And you a welcome gave,
    Flag of the Free?

Are we now cowards grown,
Flag of the Free?
Would we you now disown,
Flag of the Free?
You to whose folds we fled,
You in whose cause we bled,
Bearing you at our head,
    Flag of the Free?

Could we desert you now,
Flag of the Free,
And to black traitors bow,
Flag of the Free?
Never! through good and ill,
Ireland her blood will spill,
Bearing you onward still,
    Flag of the Free.[13]

The Era put it this way: "There is much green," they said, "mixed in with the red, white and blue."[14]

THE GERMANS

From 1840 to 1860 almost one million refugees arrived in America from the German States.[15] Crop failures and political unrest forced many to flee, and thousands settled in Williamsburg, Bushwick, East New York and New Lots.

Those who left after the abortive revolution of 1848 were known as Acht-und-vierziger (the '48ers). The newcomers worked primarily as skilled artisans in the furniture, cabinet, or piano making trades, but some became tailors and a few ran inns or hotels as they did in the old country. John Lohman established the Lohman Hotel at North Carolina (Liberty) and Wyckoff Avenues, and it became a landmark in the German community of New Lots; Lewis Altenbrand built the Railroad House at Atlantic Avenue and Vermont Street.[16]

The immigrants maintained their old world culture by using German at school, at home, and in church, where their local brebiger (preacher) issued their birth and marriage certificates. Several major forces worked harmoniously to preserve their heritage: the German press, German music, and the German language. These new Americans read their Anzeiger (Advertiser) at fier dollars preis fuer ein jahr (four dollars price for one year), or the Brooklyner Freie Presse (Brooklyn Free Press), conducted business in their native tongue, and attended meetings at their social clubs, or vereines. German-American social life centered around these organizations, which emphasized bodily strength and vigor, and fostered an interest in music, literature, or gymnastics. They held fencing or shooting matches at the Altenbrand, Bennett, or Luhrs shooting galleries (Jamaica and Bushwick Avenues), all in the Germanic tradition of gemutlichkeit, a feeling of warmth and comradeship. In 1858 seventeen well-known vereines sang publicly in New York, Hoboken, East New York, and Williamsburg.[17]

To serve the religious needs of the newcomers two new churches came into being. St. John's Evangelical Lutheran

Church, organized in the Spring of 1847, drew Protestant worshippers not only from the German population of Brownsville and Canarsie, but also from Queens County's Ozone Park and Woodhaven, most of them refugees from the German States of Mecklenburg and Schleswig-Holstein. Until 1860 German Catholics had to travel long distances for services. Under the guidance of John Laughlin of the new Brooklyn Diocese, St. Benedict's Church rose on June 30, 1860, at John Street (now Jerome Street) between Atlantic and North Carolina (now Liberty) Avenues.[18]

The immigrants made good citizens and obeyed most of the local laws, with one exception: the proscription of drinking on the Sabbath. Try as they might, no authority could keep the Germans from having their beer no matter what day of the week. German physicians often recommended beer as a legitimate dietary additive to combat anemia, athletes trained on it, and convalescents drank it to increase their appetites. To the Germans it played an important part in their culture, and they refused to amend their ways out of deference to the blue laws of their new country.[19]

They brought from their native land not only a love of drinking beer but also the expertise needed to make it. They specialized in lager, the bottom sediment brew that tasted better than traditional American products. Samuel Liebmann, a successful tavern owner in Wurttemberg, had such personal differences with his monarch, William I, that the king forbade his armed forces to frequent Liebmann's tavern or to drink his beer. Incensed by this edict, Liebmann pulled up his roots and left with his family for the new world, settling in the Bushwick, or Dutchtown (Deutschetown) section of Brooklyn.

Here he found some twenty-five brewers, mostly in the Eastern District, and almost all with Germanic names. Many of these entrepreneurs ran tiny operations, working out of the basement or one floor of a small building. Satisfying only local needs, they made deliveries in wheelbarrows or pushcarts. Most had a tap room nearby so that locals could drink the house brand and socialize. Brooklyn, a major beer producing area, had more than one hundred beer saloons listed in its city directory.[20]

Undaunted by competition, Liebmann and his three sons, Joseph, Heinrich (Henry), and Charles, bought a bankrupt brewery on Meserole Street in nearby Williamsburg and went into production. A year later they expanded, moving their operation to larger quarters at 36 Forest Street just off Bushwick Avenue. Here they thrived, buying out many of their competitors, and in 1856 they introduced their most popular brew, Rheingold.[21]

Military organizations had sprung up in East New York and Williamsburg as early as 1847, and by the time of the Civil War many immigrants had years of drill and training. The group known as the German Militia became the Kings County National Guard, and when the war began they made the transition to the army rapidly. A tent city sprang up in East New York, and the Union Place (Cypress Hills) woods served as a site for camp meetings where orators bombarded impressionable youths with rhetoric about saving the Union. Neighborhood boys responded patriotically by joining the Turner Rifles, Companies I and K of the Twentieth New York Volunteers. Dr. Albert Furgang became the physician for all of the regiments camped opposite the Howard House at Atlantic and Alabama Avenues. When Captain Bedell's

Company A of the Twenty-eighth Regiment, known as the German Rifles, marched off to fight, the entire village cheered them on.[22]

Richard L. Horsefield, a New Lots census taker, observed that "Among the Germans the war has brought out a strong sentiment of love for the Union and a determination to support the government at every sacrifice."[23]

BLACKS

In 1968 Jim Hurley, former director of the Long Island Historical Society,[24] along with engineer/pilot Joseph Haynes, pored over old Brooklyn maps seeking the remains of a once thriving black community that pre-dated the Civil War. With Haynes at the controls of a rented plane, they spotted several old houses on Bergen Street, between Rochester and Buffalo avenues. Marking them carefully on maps they returned on foot and found that they had discovered four nineteenth century farmhouses on colonial-era Hunterfly Road, the common thoroughfare that led from the hamlet of Bedford to the town of New Lots. This was the eastern corner of Weeksville, home to a black community of about one hundred families who lived in the ninth ward, an area bounded today by Eastern Parkway and Atlantic, Albany, and Ralph avenues.[25]

The former farm land, hilly and thick with woods, formed a small portion of the enormous holdings of the Lefferts family, one of Brooklyn's largest slave owners in Colonial times. In 1790 roughly forty per cent of all white families in Kings County owned at least one slave, making Kings the largest slave-holding county in New York State. The town of Bedford, for example, had seventy-two slaves out of a total population of two hundred and four. The Leffertses greeted the emancipation act of 1820 by giving or selling parcels of land to the new freedmen. It is believed that one of them, James Weeks, lent his name to the new community.[26]

In 1850, the overall Weeksville-Carrville area had a public school (Colored School 2), churches (Bethel Tabernacle African Methodist Episcopal and Baptist), an orphanage, a burial society, a home for the aged, and a cemetery. The area's census listed barbers, tailors, carpenters, painters, butchers, shoemakers, coopers, and ropemakers, skills that blacks had practiced since the seventeenth century. Susan Smith McKinney-Steward, the first black female physician in Brooklyn and the third in the nation, was born in Weeksville in 1847 on the corner of Fulton Street and Buffalo Avenue. After graduating from the New York Medical College for Women in 1870, she did post- graduate work at the Long Island Medical College Hospital and later helped found the Women's Hospital and Dispensary at Myrtle and Grand Avenues.[27]

During archaelogical digs in the 1970s, volunteers uncovered daguerreotypes hidden in attics and cellars. Some revealed well-dressed black women posing in elegant settings. Also found were family Bibles with neatly inscribed dates of births, deaths, and marriages. Other evidence pointed to the presence of the Abyssinian Daughters of Esther, a black mutual aid society started in New York in 1853 and apparently transplanted to Brooklyn. It provided for hospitalization and burial expenses for members.[28]

Blacks had lived in Brooklyn since colonial days, and many settled near today's downtown area. Tired of meeting in white churches, they started collections of fifty cents a month in order to secure facilities of their own, and in 1817 they bought two lots on the east side of High Street, between Bridge and Jay streets. In their first meeting the new church members elected Peter Croger, Benjamin Croger, Israel Jemison, John E. Jackson, and Caesar Springfield as the first trustees. In 1840 the congregation, numbering one hundred ninety-five members, bought a building at 309 Bridge Street and moved there during the pastorate of Reverend J. Morris Williams. The Reverends Richard Harvey Cain (1861-1863) and D. Dorral (1863-1866) served as ministers during the Civil War. The Bridge Street edifice became an important stop on the Underground Railroad, the loosely organized system that spirited slaves northward from southern bondage to freedom. Slaves en route to a safe destination often slept on the basement floor or hid in the cellar to keep them from Southern slave-catchers, who, under the provision of the detested 1850 Fugitive Slave Act, could legally return them to their masters. Anyone hindering a slave's capture or aiding him in any way became subject to the penalties of this regulation.[29]

Highly sensitive to slavery and its history, Brooklyn's African-American families celebrated the anniversary of black emancipation in the British West Indies each year. Large crowds would gather at the Myrtle Avenue Park each August 2nd to sing, dance and be regaled with speeches during this summer anniversary pic-nic.[30]

Although blacks worked hard, minded their own business, and made up less than two per cent of the city's population, they suffered a good deal of racial prejudice. During August 1862, a mob attacked black workers in a tobacco factory on Sedgwick Street between De Kalb and

Harrison avenues. Racial epithets spewed back and forth and the fight turned into a race riot. The neighborhood toughs tried to burn down the factory with the black workers inside, and only the timely intervention of the police kept the brawl from becoming a full-blown tragedy. The incident even appalled the anti-black Brooklyn Eagle. It ran a forceful editorial condemning the mindless and highly dangerous violence against a peaceful people. At the same time the Kings County Medical Society refused admission to a black doctor saying that they didn't want to associate with him. Many ex-slaves and freedmen who worked industriously at the Fulton Fish Market in New York, had to walk from their homes to the ferry in order to commute, as all too often they were refused admittance to the local horsecars.[31]

Brooklyn's newspapers had a decidedly anti-Negro slant. The Eagle noted that the black population of four thousand had decreased by one thousand in a decade and that "regret might not be universal as this interesting class of the population declined." It added that there had been six cases of intermarriage in all of which the woman had been "degraded." The Era used the word "nigger" freely as did the City News. The Standard asked, "What next? The darkies are looking up. The patrons of colored school Number 1 have asked the Board of Education to appoint a white teacher in their school as they desire to have their pupils brought up like other folk's children. What next? The Reverend H.W. Beecher is not only advocating freedom with equality but also amalgamation."[32]

Despite the obvious racist attitudes of most Brooklyn newspapers, the city still had a favorable reputation among blacks. In 1861 William Wells Brown, a journalist for the New York Anglo-African, reported that Brooklyn offered plenty of opportunity for improving the "temporal, the social and the intellectual condition of colored men as any place in the country."[33]

During the fourth month of the Civil War the Eagle rendered a great disservice when Frederick Douglass, the former slave and the most influential black leader of the mid-nineteenth century, spoke in Brooklyn. Douglass suggested that black men be given the chance to fight for their country in return for citizenship rights. The Eagle ridiculed his idea and wrote scornfully, "Douglass is trying to get the darkies to take a hand in the war. He says that the war is for slavery and to let the blacks, with their sinewy arms, fight the battle. We can only put down insurrection, he adds, by putting down slavery. The gen'man ob color don't take the hint. If there is any fighting to be done, Sambo, as a general thing, desires to be counted out. The genius of the darkey is of a culinary and not a military character. He takes to waiting on tables, white-washing, barbering, cooking and other useful and honorable occupations as naturally as a duck to water but he has a wholesale dread of gunpowder."[34]

The Standard reminded Douglass that conferring citizenship did not rest with the federal government but rather with the individual states and that New York, in a plebiscite three years earlier, had voted down Negro suffrage by over one hundred thousand votes.[35]

Of course, more than one hundred eighty thousand blacks put the lie to the Eagle's slander by enlisting in the Union armies and fighting bravely when allowed to do so. Among them were David and Emanuel Holmes, Canarsie fishermen. David became a sergeant in Company E of the Twentieth Regiment of the New York State Colored Troops, and Emanuel served in Company F of the Twenty-sixth United States Colored Infantry. Emanuel lost two toes as a result of wounds he sustained. Both men are buried in Canarsie Cemetery, and their descendants still live just blocks away. [36] Five Brooklyn blacks also served with the famous Fifty-fourth Massachusetts Volunteer Infantry Regiment recently featured in the movie Glory. They were Peter Vogelsang (Stanton Place), Henry B. Marshall, John A. Green, Richard Seaman (Skillman near Lorimer), and Samuel Moles.[37]

On July 23, 1863, Vogelsang received gunshot wounds in his left chest during a battle at St. John's Island in South Carolina. After eight weeks of recuperation, he returned to duty. In early 1865 protests from blacks and prominent Northerners led to a policy of promoting blacks, and the lantern-jawed Vogelsang, a clerk in civilian life, used his skills to become quartermaster sergeant and then first lieutenant, one of only three blacks from the Fifty-fourth to be commissioned. After receiving his discharge on August 20, 1865, he returned to Brooklyn, where he resided at 43 Hull Street and worked as a messenger. Green, a former farmer, and Moles, a laborer in civilian life, both sustained wounds during the storming of Fort Wagner, South Carolina, in July 1863.[38]

The Bureau for Colored Troops, established in May 1863, had so many volunteers that they created the category of United States Colored Troops (U.S.C.T.). Soon this new grouping included all but one Connecticut and three Massachusetts regiments. The federal government appointed white officers and chose chaplains to minister to the new black soldiers. Out of the one hundred thirty-three chaplains, only fourteen were black, and one, George S. LeVere, came from Brooklyn. Formerly the pastor of Saint Paul's Congregational Church on Myrtle Avenue, he served as chaplain for the Twentieth Regiment, U.S.C.T. LeVere wrote regularly to the Philadelphia <u>Christian Recorder</u>, giving glimpses of daily life in a black regiment: consoling sick and wounded soldiers, counseling those who had problems at home, and teaching many of the new freedmen to read and write. Le Vere also helped with mail delivery, wrote letters of condolence to grieving families, and forwarded effects of dead soldiers to their homes. At the war's end he remained in the south to work with former slaves, and helped found several churches in the Knoxville, Tennessee, area.[39]

THE JEWS

In 1845 a small group of Alsatian Jews moved from New York to Grand Street in the town of Williamsburg. Tired of riding back and forth on the ferry to attend religious services in Manhattan, they decided to form their own synagogue, Brooklyn's first. Starting in Moses Kessel's home on North 2nd Street the Israelites [40] later rented a hall down the block for one hundred fifty dollars a year. The new congregation called their <u>shul</u> (synagogue) Baith Israel Ansher Emes, and the official papers filed in Kings County clerk's office in 1856 lists the following founding fathers: Morris Ehrlich, Marcus Bass, Isaac Jones, Nehemiah Hofheimer, Tagol Samter, Michael Price, and Joshua Mendes. Although the temple prospered over the years, a group of dissidents decided in 1861 to break away and form an offshoot synagogue that would be known as Beth Elohim. On September 29, 1861, a group of prominent businessmen led by Bernard Schellenberg met at Grenada Hall on Myrtle Avenue and drew up plans for their new enterprise. Others in attendance were Levi Blumenau, Moses Hess, Alois Lazansky, S. Rosenberg, Raphael Strauss, Solomon Stern, and Abraham Wechsler. The group elected Moses Hess president and appointed Reverend George Brandenstein rabbi. They raised six thousand dollars to purchase the Calvary Protestant Episcopal Church on Pearl Street between Concord and Nassau streets and dedicated this building on March 30, 1862.[41]

Many of the former Alsatians went into the cattle and feed business, as they had practiced these trades in the old country. Aaron Levy ran an abbatoir on Hudson Street and became one of the richest Jews in Brooklyn. These slaughterhouses, located on Johnson Street, would become the hub of the kosher meat market in Kings County.[42]

Abraham Abraham, son of a wealthy merchant, learned the retail trade in a family store in Newark, New Jersey,[43] and on Valentine's Day in 1865, he and Joseph Wechsler opened a dry goods store at 275 Fulton Street. They felt assured that with hard work and a good deal of personal attention to their clients they would be successful. The formula paid off. Since they had only three helpers, the partners pitched in by dressing the window and sweeping up. Located in the center of Brooklyn's mercantile district their establishment opened at 8 a.m. and closed at 7 p.m. and home delivery was offered on any item, even a single spool of thread. Reminiscing fifty years later, after his store had become A&S (Abraham and Straus), Abraham said wryly that hoop skirts, bigger and bigger with each year, made it difficult for some clients to even enter his store![44]

One day while strolling through the Heights, Abraham saw a bust of President Lincoln in a barber shop window. He bought it from the proprietor and took it home. In April 1865, as the city mourned the assassinated president, Abraham took the bust, draped it with black crepe and placed it in his store's front window. It became a conversation piece, being the only one like it in the entire city.[45]

Since Jews did not list themselves as such on the passenger lists, they cannot be as readily identified as the Irish and German immigrants. Perhaps two hundred fifty Jewish families lived in Brooklyn during the Civil War era, but this is only a guess based upon traditionally Jewish names listed in the city directory. In 1861 eighteen Levis or Levys, and eleven Cohns or Cohens appear among other Jewish sounding names near Court, Fulton, Columbia and Hicks streets and Atlantic, Myrtle, and DeKalb avenues. In the Eastern District's Williamsburg they settled along Johnson Avenue, South 1st, South 4th, South 7th, and Grand streets. Some owned dry goods stores or made segars (cigars) or umbrellas. Levi Blumenau, who came from the German states in 1845, established a real estate business. Moses Loewenthal (32 Hudson Street), Abraham Marks (81 Main Street), Samuel Oppenheimer (Franklin Street), and Bernhard Schnellenberg (119 Myrtle Avenue), ran merchant tailor shops. Schnellenberg, originally from Frankfurt, made uniforms for the Fourteenth Regiment. James Gru manufactured men's hats on Atlantic

Avenue, near the East River. Real-estate agent Solomon Furst (410 Atlantic Avenue), joined New York State Militia's Second Cavalry Regiment and saw action during the famous Draft Riots of 1863. Lieutenant-Colonel Leopold Newman of Congregation Ansher Emes (21 Fulton Street), fought with the Army of the Potomac. Severely wounded at the battle of Fredericksburg, he died in a Washington hospital on June 7, 1863. Prussian-born Coleman Cohen enlisted in the Thirteenth Regiment, became a captain, and sustained wounds in the first battle of Bull Run. He survived his injuries and lived until 1933.[46]

The Civil War and its threat to the Union proved a strong incentive for the Irish, German and Jewish immigrants to display their patriotism, giving them an important common enthusiasm to share with their more well-established neighbors. Blacks showed that they could and would fight for their country even though it treated them as second class citizens. In doing so they planted a seed that would one day grow into greater equality.

[1] Pessen, Edward, Riches, Class and Power Before the Civil War(Lexington, Mass.,1973), pp. 109,207,209.
Brooklyn Almanac, p.31.
[2] Schoenbaum, Eleonora, Emerging Neighborhoods and the Development of Brooklyn Fringe Areas, 1850-1930, doctoral dissertation, Columbia University, N.Y., 1977, p.4.
[3] Political Nativism in Brooklyn, Richard J. Purcell and John F. Poole, American Irish Historical Society Journal, Vol. XXXII(New York, 1941), pp.11,12.
[4] Political Nativism in Brooklyn, pp.11,12,15.

McCaffrey, Lawrence J., <u>The Irish Diaspora in America</u> (Bloomington, Ind., 1976), p.68

Ernst, Robert, <u>Immigrant Life in New York City</u>(Port Washington, N.Y., 1949), p.135.

Shannon, William V., <u>The American Irish</u>(N.Y., 1966), p.27,p.40.

[5] Armbruster, Eugene, <u>Brooklyn's Eastern District</u>(Brooklyn, N.Y., 1942), p.13.

Victory, James J., <u>The Promise at the Doorstep</u>, master's degree dissertation, St. John's University, 1979, introduction.

[6] <u>The City of Brooklyn, A Political History</u>, pp.18,19,33.

<u>Immigrant Life in New York City</u>, p.51.

<u>The Irish Diaspora in America</u>, pp.67,68.

Wittke, Carl, <u>We Who Built America</u>,(Cleveland,1939),p.134.

O'Connell, J.C., <u>The Irish in the Revolution and the Civil War</u>(Washington, D.C., 1903), p.23.

<u>The American Irish</u>, p.27,39.

<u>Brooklyn Almanac</u>, p.31.

[7] <u>The Promise at the Doorstep</u>, pp.11,56.

<u>The American Irish</u>, p.39.

[8] <u>Promise at the Doorstep</u>, introduction.

[9] When the advertisements did not say "Irish need not apply."

[10] Joyce, William L., <u>Editors and Ethnicity, A History of the Irish-American Press 1848-1883</u>, doctoral dissertation, University of Michigan(Ann Arbor, 1974),p.35.

<u>The American Irish</u>, pp.54-56.

McPherson, James M.,<u>The Negro's Civil War</u>(New York,1965), p.70.

[11] <u>The American Irish</u>, p.56.

[12] <u>The American Irish</u>, pp.55,58,59.

Conyngham, D.P., <u>The Irish Brigade</u>(N.Y.,1867), p.12.

Brooklyn <u>Standard</u>, July 6,1861.

Gibson, Florence E., <u>The Attitudes of the New York Irish Toward the State and National Affairs 1848-1892</u>(N.Y., 1951), p.122.

<u>Some Pre-Civil War Irish Militiamen of Brooklyn</u>, William Harper Bennett, <u>The American Irish Historical Society Journal</u>, Vol. XXI, 1922, pp.172,173.

[13] Scott, John Anthony, <u>The Ballad of America</u>(N.Y.,1966), p.224,225.

[14] Brooklyn <u>Era</u>, December 28,1861.

[15] <u>Immigrant Life in New York</u>, p.1.

[16] <u>Immigrant Life in New York</u>, pp.102,103,112.

Landesman, Alter F., <u>A History of New Lots</u>(Port Washington, N.Y., 1977), pp.101,102.

Miller, Eugene and Steinlage, Forrest, <u>Der Turner Soldat</u>(Louisville, Ky.,1988), p.7.

[17] <u>The City of Brooklyn A Political History</u>, pp.12,19.

Brooklyn <u>Eagle</u>, March 21, 1934.

Wald, Ralph Forster, <u>Brooklyn Is America</u>(New York,1950), pp.19,86,87.

Heidenreich, Frederick J., <u>Old Days and Old Ways in East New York</u>(Brooklyn, 1948), pp.19,20.

<u>A History of New Lots</u>, p.102,112.

<u>Immigrant Life in New York City</u>, pp.112,130.

[18] <u>A History of New Lots</u>, pp.106,107.

[19] History of the Liebmann family, microfiche, B.H.S.

<u>Old Days and Old Ways in East New York</u>, pp.19,20.

<u>Beer in the American Home</u>, Eloise Davison, pamphlet,

B.H.S., N.Y., 1937.

[20] Beer in the American Home.

History of the Liebmann family, B.H.S.

Brooklyn City Directory, 1860.

Anderson, Will, The Breweries of Brooklyn(Croton Falls, 1976), pp.100,102.

[21] History of the Liebmann family, B.H.S.

Breweries of Brooklyn, pp.100,102.

[22] History of New Lots, pp. 105,139.

Brooklyn Is America, p.88.

Brooklyn Eagle, April 25,1861.

[23] History of New Lots, pp. 138.

[24] Now the Brooklyn Historical Society.

[25] Brooklyn's Eastern District, p.45.

Weeksville Then and Now, pamphlet, edited by Joan Maynard and Gwen Cottman, Brooklyn, undated.

Weeksville Curriculum Unit, Project Weeksville, directed by Barbara D. Jackson, Brooklyn, 1971.

[26] Weeksville Then and Now.

Slavery on Long Island, a Study of Economic Motivation, Ralph R. Ireland, Journal of Long Island History, Vol. VI, Spring 1966, no. 2., p.2.

McCullough, David, Brooklyn and How it Got That Way(New York, 1983), p.17.

McManus, Edgar J., A History of Negro Slavery in New York(Syracuse, 1966), p.42.

Connolly, Harold X., A Ghetto Grows in Brooklyn(New York, 1977), pp.4,8.

Weeksville Historical Research Review, The Pieces of a Puzzle, by Robert J. Swan, 1971,pp.2,21

[27] <u>People of Brooklyn</u>, David S. Ment and Mary S. Donovan, pamphlet, Brooklyn Discovery, Brooklyn Educational and Cultural Alliance, Brooklyn, 1980, B.H.S., pp. 17,18.
<u>A Ghetto Grows in Brooklyn</u>, pp.8,23.
<u>Weeksville Curriculum Unit</u>.
<u>Brooklyn Almanac</u>, p.31.

[28] <u>Weeksville Then and Now</u>
<u>Weeksville Curriculum Unit</u>, p.7.
<u>The Pieces of a Puzzle</u>, p.9.

[29] <u>A Ghetto Grows in Brooklyn</u>, p.10.
Jordan, Amos, <u>Compiled History of the African Wesleyan Methodist Episcopal Church</u>, 1973, B.H.S.

[30] Brooklyn <u>Eagle</u>, August 2,1861. 1860 spelling.

[31] New York <u>Times</u> August 5, 1862.
<u>The Negro's Civil War</u>, p.70.
<u>Brooklyn and How It Got That Way</u>, p.36.

[32] Brooklyn <u>Eagle</u>, March 8, 1861.
Brooklyn <u>City News</u>, March 22, 1864.
Brooklyn <u>Standard</u>, July 11, 1863.
Shroth, Raymond, <u>The Eagle and Brooklyn</u> (Westport,Ct.,1974), p.61

[33] <u>A Ghetto Grows in Brooklyn</u>, p.22.

[34] Brooklyn <u>Eagle</u>, August 28, 1861.

[35] Brooklyn <u>Standard</u>, February 28, 1863.

[36] Boatner, Mark III, <u>The Civil War Dictionary</u>(N.Y.,1959), p.584.
Interview with the Holmes family.
<u>The Brooklyn Neighborhood Book</u>, edited by Nanette Rainone, Brooklyn,1985, p.28.

[37] Emilio, Luis F., <u>Brave Black Regiment</u>(New York, 1894), pp.355,358,366.

Greene, Robert Ewell, <u>Black Defenders of America 1775-1973</u>(Chicago, 1974), p.96.

[38] <u>Brave Black Regiment</u>, pp. 315-317,339,358,366.

<u>Black Defenders of America</u>, p.96.

Service record of Peter Vogelsang, author's collection.

<u>The Black Military Experience</u>, edited by Ira Berlin, New York, 1982, p.308.

[39] Service record, George S. LeVere, author's collection.

<u>Black Chaplains in the Union Army</u>, Edwin S. Redkey, <u>Civil War History</u>, vol.33, December 1987, pp.331,337,349.

<u>Negro History Bulletin</u>, vol.27, October 1963-November,1964.

[40] Newspapers called Jews "Israelites" and "believers in the Faith of Abraham."

[41] Union Temple of Brooklyn, 100th year commemorative bro chure, New York Public Library,(hereafter N.Y.P.L.).

Abelow, Samuel P., <u>History of Brooklyn Jewry</u>(Brooklyn, 1937), pp.5,14,15,23,24.

[42] <u>Brooklyn Is America</u>, pp.102-104.

[43] Two of his fellow clerks were Simon Bloomingdale and Benjamin Altman.

[44] Abraham and Straus 80th year anniversary brochure, 1865-1945.

[45] <u>Ibid</u>.

In 1893 Isadore and Nathan Straus bought out Joseph Wechsler and the new partners called their store Abraham and Straus (A.& S.).

[46] Brooklyn <u>Standard</u>, June 10,1863.

<u>History of Brooklyn Jewry</u>, pp.5-11.

<u>Brooklyn Is America</u>, pp.102,104.

Brooklyn <u>Daily Union</u>, August 1,1863.

THE NEIGHBORHOODS

The city's most prestigious neighborhood, Brooklyn Heights, sat on a bluff directly across from Manhattan Island and offered a magnificent view of the great harbor, Staten Island's rolling hills, and New Jersey's nearby woods. This premier location made a strong impression on New York's noted diarist George Templeton Strong, who wrote, "The situation on the Heights overlooking the bay can hardly be matched in any great city in Christendom. How often have I wished I could exchange this house for one of them and that I could see from my library windows that noble prospect and that wide open expanse of sky and the going down of the sun every evening."[1]

Until department store magnate A. T. Stewart built his "palace" on 5th Avenue and 34th Street in New York, Henry C. Bowen owned the most luxurious mansion in the metropolitan area, a prime example of Colonial architecture. Located on Willow Street overlooking the Narrows, his lavish home served as a mecca for visiting luminaries, including Massachusetts Senator Charles Sumner and two of New York's most influential newspaper men, editors Horace Greeley of the Tribune and Henry J. Raymond of the Times. When the Hungarian freedom fighter Louis Kossuth arrived in America, he, too, spent time in Bowen's home.[2]

Originally an area of large estates with neatly manicured lawns, gardens, and orchards, the Heights was home to the city's first families, those who set the standards for manners and culture in Brooklyn. Hezekiah Pierrepont, the largest landowner, divided his sixty acres and sold plots to "genteel people who wanted to live in a select neighborhood." And select it became. Brooklyn's elite responded enthusiastically, and joining the Remsens, Middaghs, and DeBevoises were men like A. A. Low (3 Pierrepont Street), the great tea importer and owner of China Trade clipper ships, and businessman Leonard Jerome, founder of the Coney Island Jockey Club, who would one day join with financier August Belmont in horse-racing enterprises. Jerome's daughter, Jennie, born at 197 Amity Street, married into an old English family. Her son, Winston Churchill, became one of England's most illustrious prime ministers.[3]

Brooklyn's merchant princes chose the Heights for business reasons, too. A brief stroll north would take them to the efficient East River ferries and a five-minute ride to their Manhattan offices; if they walked south, they could easily visit the piers where their trading vessels lay at anchor.[4]

Fortunately for the Heights, the real estate boom in the early nineteenth century veered to the south and east leaving it largely undisturbed by the wheeling and dealing of speculators and builders. Of some eleven hundred homes in the area today, more than half stood prior to the Civil War.[5]

The neighborhood had many fine hotels, too, including the Pierrepont House,"a very spacious and elegant establishment" on Montague Terrace overlooking the Wall Street ferry landing; the Mansion House on Henry and Pierrepont Streets, which furnished "elegant accomodations" for some two hundred fifty guests; and the Globe, 244 Fulton Street, which offered omnibus service every five minutes. The Nassau Hotel, at Nassau and Hudson, touted their American and English ale on draught "from four taps at all hours," brandies, wines, segars,[6] and oysters of "the choicest kinds and in every style of cuisine." They also featured billiards. Deson's Hotel at 160 Fulton Street offered single and double rooms from two dollars to seven dollars per week, with dinner served from 12 to 3 p.m. Their specialty was ice cream and Philadelphia lager beer and ale.[7]

In addition to its many fine hotels, the Heights served as Brooklyn's cultural center. The Athenaeum (Atlantic Avenue and Clinton Street), founded in 1853 to promote the "moral and intellectual interests of the youth of the city," boasted an excellent library, and its reading and lecture rooms offered fine entertainment. Many prominent figures of the day spoke there, including Ralph Waldo Emerson and humorist Artemis Ward. The Lyceum, at Washington and Concord Streets, also enjoyed an excellent reputation as a literary institute.[8]

The city planners had grandiose schemes for nearby Atlantic Avenue, the city's widest thoroughfare. They envisioned an ornamental avenue replicating Paris's Champs Elysee, with sidewalks on both sides, huge shady trees, and a railroad line running down the middle. The entire width of this magnificent boulevard would be fully macadamized, and no doubt rival the finest streets in any American metropolis.[9]

Other neighborhoods, too, held a special place in Brooklyn's heart. Flatbush (Dutch T Vlacke Bos - wooded plain) had the largest collection of Dutch farmhouses on the East Coast, like the Wyckoff-Bennett Homestead at 1669 East 22nd Street, which still stands today. These sturdy buildings had a central chimney with a storage-space loft, with low roofs which merged the second story into the front porch. Some had tiny twelve-paned windows, white shingles and blue shutters, with attic rafters held down by wooden pegs. A very few still had extra small windows, used as a precaution against Indian raids in the early eighteenth century. Flatbush had several roads leading directly to the ocean, and its residents saw many a horse race held on them. The famous Vanderveer windmill stood not far away in Flatlands, and to the south a small neighborhood called Sheeps Head Bay [10] featured seafood dinners. [11]

The hamlet of Bedford thrived once the horse car trolley reached its borders. Almost half of its residents owned their own homes and workingmen could now live in this country site and commute to work. The neighborhood, made up of Brooklynites from primarily Irish and German backgrounds, grew steadily. William Payne, an English architect and decorator, owned one of the more pretentious homes there, with a lawn large enough to set up a croquet field. His house, in the midst of farm land in 1860, became 22 Halsey Street after the war and remained standing until 1905. [12]

[1] The Diary of George Templeton Strong, edited by Allen Nevins and Milton H. Thomas(New York, 1952), 4 vol., vol.4, pp.565,566.

Lancaster, Clay, Old Brooklyn Heights(Rutland, Vt., 1961), p.13.

Callender, James H., Yesterdays on Brooklyn Heights(N.Y., 1927),p.13.

[2] Old Brooklyn Heights, p.17.

The City of Brooklyn, A Political History, p.17.

Freeman, Andrew, Mr. Lincoln Goes To New York(N.Y., 1960), p.63.

Yesterdays on Brooklyn Heights, p.150.

[3] Riches, Class and Power Before the Civil War, p.109.

Martin, Ralph G., Jenny(Englewood Cliffs, 1977, p.30.

Big Apple Almanac, edited by Patrick M. Reynolds, Willow Street, Pa.

New York A Guide to the Metropolis, p.338.

[4] Riches, Class and Power Before the Civil War, p.180.

[5] New York, A Guide to the Metropolis, pp. 155,299,354.

[6] 1860 spelling.

[7] Brooklyn Evening Star, April 10, 1861.

[8] Miller's New York As It Is, pp. 100,112,113.

[9] Manual for the Common Council of the City of Brooklyn, 1863, pp. 139,140.

[10] 1860 spelling.

[11] Dolkart, Andrew S., This Is Brooklyn(Brooklyn, 1990), p.84.

Ford, James L., Brooklyn in the 1860's, New York Herald, May 31, 1925.

[12] Emerging Neighborhoods, p.38.

Younger, William Lee, Old Brooklyn in Early Photographs(New York, 1978), p.77.

THE CHURCHES

During the Civil War era Protestant houses of worship predominated in Brooklyn, and the most famous by far, the Plymouth Church, had as its spiritual leader the flamboyant Henry Ward Beecher, who at times preached to more than fifteen hundred people at a single service. Although it seemed to some that the Plymouth Church held the copyright on religion in Brooklyn, the 1861 city directory listed seventeen Baptist, fifteen Congregationalist, twenty-five Protestant Episcopal, twenty-five Methodist Episcopal, three Methodist Protestant, nineteen Presbyterian, fifteen Reformed Dutch, twenty Roman Catholic, four Universalist, and ten miscellaneous churches, and one synagogue.[1]

Nahor Staples served as pastor for the Second Unitarian Church of the Savior at Pierrepont Street and Monroe Place. Soon after the bombardment of Fort Sumter signalling the beginning of the war, his congregants sent a huge box filled with warm winter clothing to Union forces, and church women patiently scraped lint from old linen to be used to dress wounds. Staples and his parishioners specialized in this type of public service, something that gained them a left-handed compliment from some of their neighbors who saw the Unitarian Church as a place "where there were so many good works and so little faith."[2]

Saint John's Episcopal Church, the first of its denomination in Kings County outside of the city of Brooklyn, held its consecration services on July 16, 1835, in the town of New Utrecht. Located then, as now, at 9818 Fort Hamilton Parkway, it catered to the religious needs of the soldiers at

Fort Hamilton. Thomas Jonathan (Stonewall) Jackson and Robert E. Lee, both of whom would win everlasting fame during the Civil War, worshipped there during the 1840s.[3]

Weeksville's and Carrville's black churches became focal points of community life, involved in social and economic problems as well as religious needs. Many black churches, like the Bridge Street African Wesleyan Methodist Episcopal Church, incorporated in 1818, became stations on the Underground Railroad. The Siloan Presbyterian (1847) and the Concord Baptist (1848) stood near the present-day downtown area of Brooklyn, while the Bethel Tabernacle African Methodist Episcopal was on the corner of Schenectady Avenue and Dean Street.[4]

Fort Hamilton's Irish and German soldiers helped establish Saint Patrick's Roman Catholic Church in 1849, turning it into a lone outpost of Catholic worship in New Utrecht. Previously, mass had been held in parishioners' barns or homes whenever a priest became available. Cummin's barn, behind Albert Johnson's house, often accommodated the faithful for mass as the nearest Catholic church lay ten miles to the north, in Brooklyn proper. The diocese finally took form in 1853 under Bishop John Laughlin, of 190 Jay Street, who continued to lead it until 1891.[5]

Connecticut's most celebrated minister, Lyman Beecher, had two children who left indelible marks on America during the Civil War era. His daughter, Harriet Beecher Stowe, wrote the most popular and controversial book of the day, Uncle Tom's Cabin, and his son Henry, became the country's most illustrious preacher.[6]

The thirty-three-year old Henry Ward Beecher became

the spiritual leader of the pioneer Congregationalist Plymouth church in Brooklyn in 1847. Neither the church nor the city would ever be the same again. His extraordinary sermons drew such unprecedented crowds, including many who came from New York on the Fulton Street Ferry (dubbed "Beecher's Ferry"), that his new church could not properly accommodate them. When it burned down in 1849 a new and more spacious edifice took its place on Orange Street near Hicks.[7]

Beecher spiced everyday language with local slang and laced his homilies with humor, unusual for a preacher of that day. His sermons included a range of subjects: temperance, suffrage, reform, phrenology, slavery, anti-slavery, and the impending war. His style of presentation seemed just like normal conversation and his ability to communicate enabled him to establish a strong empathy with churchgoers without being authoritarian. One listener compared Beecher's technique with that of Edward Everett, the leading orator of that day, and the speaker who preceded Abraham Lincoln at Gettysburg in November 1863. Everett, he said, reminded him of a "peacefully flowing river in which was reflected the beautiful images of the flowers and foliage upon its banks." Beecher's style, however, resembled that of "a mountain torrent rushing wildly along carrying everything before it by its very impetuosity and force."[8]

Beecher also presided over a highly efficient organization. Even though as many as fifteen hundred worshippers might attend a single service, his eight deacons, performing the sacrament each communion day, distributed bread and wine to all in less than ten minutes.[9] Plymouth Church members, many originally from New England, grew in numbers from twenty-three in 1847 to three hundred forty-three in 1850. Seven years later twelve hundred Congregationalists claimed membership, with a waiting list of more than two thousand. As the largest public hall in Brooklyn, the church served also as an important meeting place. Over the years it featured such famous speakers as William Makepeace Thackeray, Charles Dickens, Ralph Waldo Emerson, Josh Billings, and Artemis Ward. The church also served as a pulpit for anti- slavery advocates -- Wendell Phillips, William Lloyd Garrison, John Greenleaf Whittier, Charles Sumner -- yet Beecher himself was not enamored with their methods. In particular he found Garrison's "screaming" undignified, futile, and counterproductive. Any mind-change concerning slavery, he felt, would come about through moderate, Beecher-like persuasion, something that, unfortunately, vanished overnight with his involvement in the aftermath of the Kansas-Nebraska Act.[10]

The Kansas-Nebraska Act, passed in 1854 and based on Illinois Senator Stephen A. Douglas's concept of popular sovereignty, provided that both Kansas and Nebraska be organized into territories on the basis of an election to determine the status of slavery. As settlers rushed westward to cast their votes, Kansas became a bloody battleground of rival factions. The soon-to-be infamous John Brown and his sons hacked to death pro-slavery men at Pottawatamie in the "name of freedom," and Missouri "border ruffians" plundered Lawrence, Kansas,"for slavery." The civil warfare, although contained in 1859, continued sporadically for the next two years, adding greatly to the tension between the north and south that caused the Civil War.[11]

Beecher involved himself inadvertently in the slavery fray while attending a meeting in New Haven, Connecticut, on March 22, 1856. He learned that a contingent of New Englanders was heading west to settle in Kansas in order to cast their votes for an anti-slavery ticket. They needed weapons for protection, and in the heat of the moment Beecher rashly pledged the Plymouth Church to provide twenty-five rifles to promote a "just solution" of the western problems. His gesture resulted in great embarrassment as the press singled him out as a radical, based solely on his newly acquired fame. Beecher's contribution to the abolitionist cause to that point had been minor, yet the promised weapons suddenly become "Beecher's Bibles" and his bailiwick the "Church of the Holy Rifles."[12]

Vexed and somewhat astonished by this reaction, Beecher turned his boundless energy toward a more dramatic demonstration of his showmanship; he would "auction off" a slave. In late May 1856, he arranged to have a small mulatto woman brought from a plantation near Staunton, Virginia, and he "sold" her to his congregation in a mock auction. While many questioned the authenticity of the arrangements, there remained little doubt of its impact on Beecher's flock. After his sermon and the final hymn, Beecher called the twenty-two-year-old slave, Sarah, to his pulpit. Sarah walked slowly, head bowed, and took a seat near the famous minister. She lifted her eyes, stared at the spellbound audience, and burst into sobs. Her plight tugged at the heart of the most stolid Congregationalist as Beecher's inflamed rhetoric described her life. Daughter of a well-known white citizen, she had been put up for sale by her own father. The slave dealer involved contacted Beecher through a mutual friend and they struck a deal allowing Sarah to go north with the promise of either her return or the full manumission fee.[13]

Beecher's description of her plight and his demand for "bids" for the young woman unleashed a frenzy of generosity amid tears, sobs and shrieks. Twenty-dollar notes were stuffed into the collection boxes and many tore bracelets, necklaces and watches from their person and forced them on the hard-pressed ushers. For half an hour contributions poured in, eight hundred thirty-three dollars in all, far more than was needed to buy Sarah's freedom.[14]

Four years later, on February 5, 1860, Beecher's congregation bought freedom for Sally Maria Diggs. Known as "Pink," her one-sixteenth African blood qualified her for a life of slavery in the south. The youngster, about nine, as white as any of the children of Beecher's church members, was the daughter of a prominent Washington, D.C. physician. Born into slavery in Port Tobacco, Maryland, she saw all of her family sold further south with the exception of her grandmother, with whom she lived. Her owner, however, decided to sever even this arrangement and sell her for nine hundred dollars. Her predicament came to the attention of a young Episcopal seminarian, John Falkner Blake, of Alexandria, Virginia, and he contacted Beecher. Blake gave a bond guaranteeing either the nine hundred dollars or Pink's return, and she traveled to Brooklyn. In another emotional outburst, Beecher's flock contributed as much toward Pink's manumission as they had for Sarah. Later Pink changed her name to Rose Ward Diggs in honor of Rose Terry, a local poet who contributed a valuable ring, and Henry Ward Beecher, who had made her freedom possible.[15]

Blake received the money and went through the legalities necessary to free Pink. He first had to purchase her himself and then officially manumit her. The following is a copy of the papers he filed.

*   *   *   *

Whereas on the fifth day of February in the year of our Lord eighteen hundred and sixty the Reverend Henry Ward Beecher of the city of Brooklyn state of New York presented to the congregation of said city of which congregation he is the pastor the case of Sally Maria Diggs, usually called Pink who was then a slave child offered for sale in the city of Washington District of Columbia and whereas the said Beecher and congregation were desirous that the said slave child should be set free in order that she might not be separated from her grandmother with whom she had lived up to that date and

Whereas a contribution of money was made by the said congregation on the date above mentioned for the purpose of securing the freedom of the said slave child which money was put into my hand by the said Beecher with instructions to take the proper steps for securing the freedom of the said slave child and

Whereas on the eighth day of February in the year of our Lord eighteen hundred and sixty in pursuance of said instructions I did purchase the said slave from the owner John C. Cook of the city of Washington D.C. for the sum of nine hundred dollars and received from the said Cook a bill of sale of the said slave to myself and

Whereas the said slave child is now my legal property

53

Now be it known that I John Falkner Blake now residing in the city of Alexandria in the State of Virginia for divers and good causes and considerations me thereto moving have releived (sic) from slavery liberated manumitted and set free and by these presents to hereby release from slavery manumit and set free my mulatto girl named Sally Maria Diggs commonly called "Pink" aged about nine years and able to work and gain a sufficient livelihood and maintenance and her the said Mulatto girl named Sally Maria Diggs I do declare to be henceforth free manumitted and forever discharged from all manner of servitude or service to me- my executors administrators heirs and assigns forever.

In testimony whereof I have hereto set my hand and seal this eleventh day of February one thousand eight hundred and sixty

*   *   *   *   *   *

City and County of Washington
District of Columbia
On this eleventh day of February one thousand eight hundred and sixty before me a justice of the peace is and for said city county and district came personally the above named John Falkner Blake and being known to me as the person who executed the above deed of manumission and duly acknowledged the instrument of manumission to be his act and deed for the purpose therein mentioned.

Thomas Donn (seal)
Justice of the Peace[16]

*   *   *   *

On May 27, 1927, during the Plymouth Church's 80th year, an event took place that rivaled in excitement anything that Henry Ward Beecher ever conjured up. During a special Sunday evening service, an elderly, light skinned black woman walked slowly to the pulpit to be introduced to a cheering audience. The wife of a prominent Washington, D.C., attorney named James Hunt, she had been, sixty-seven years earlier, a slave child named Sally Maria Diggs. Pink, the former slave, had returned to Brooklyn to honor the memory of her benefactor.[17]

Shortly after recovering from the "sale" of Pink, the Plymouth Church looked forward to a visit from Illinois attorney Abraham Lincoln. In the fall of 1859 the men's club, trying to fill two slots in their speaking schedule, asked lecture agent James A. Briggs to gain Lincoln's services. Briggs sent off a telegram saying: "Will you speak in Mr. Beecher's Church Brooklyn on or about the 29th of November on any subject you please pay 200 dollars."[18]

The future president, so impressive in his debates with Stephen Douglas in the senatorial race of 1858, had enjoyed little luck with lecturing. One talk, on "discovery and invention," went poorly, and another had to be cancelled because of lack of attendance. Lincoln, however, recognized this offer as a golden opportunity. He could speak to a sophisticated eastern audience in Brooklyn, the nation's third largest city, and gain publicity for both himself and his philosophy. His law partner, William Herndon, believed "it would open the way to the presidency." Lincoln decided to accept.[19]

He inquired if a late February appearance and a talk on a political subject would do. If so, he could speak and then go north to visit his eldest son Robert at Phillips Academy in

Exeter, New Hampshire.[20] Upon receiving an affirmative reply, Lincoln set to work as never before preparing what he thought might be the most important speech of his life. Lincoln pored over the back issues of New York Tribune editorials, spent hours making notes on items in the Congressional Globe, and looked as though he would memorize Elliott's Debates on the Federal Constitution. His subject - the Founding Fathers' attitude toward slavery.[21]

When Lincoln left Springfield, Illinois, in late February, he thought his final destination would be the Plymouth Church in Brooklyn. On arrival, though, he learned that the sponsorship of his talk had been taken over by the Young Men's Central Republican Union of New York, a group opposed to Senator William H. Seward, the front runner for the 1860 Republican presidential nomination. Lincoln would now make his presentation at Cooper Union in New York on Monday, February 27. This relatively new seat of learning specialized in political presentations to enlighten the public. An advertisement in the New York Times announced: "Hon. Abraham Lincoln, of Illinois, will speak at the Cooper Institute on Mon Evening Feb 27 to the Republicans of New York."[22]

Concerned that feelings might be hurt, Lincoln visited the Plymouth Church on Sunday, February 26, and sat in pew number 89, near the front of the left center aisle. After services he received a dinner invitation from Henry Bowen, an invitation he declined, explaining that he needed the time to polish the speech he was to give the next evening.[23]

The beardless, fifty-one-year-old Lincoln arrived at Cooper Union the next night in the middle of a snowstorm.

He shared the dais with New York <u>Post</u> editor William Cullen Bryant, prominent lawyer David Dudley Field, and New York <u>Tribune</u> publisher Horace Greeley, all enemies of Seward and the senator's chief henchman, political boss and Albany editor Thurlow Weed.[24]

Fifteen hundred people each paid twenty-five cents to hear the "westerner." The lanky Lincoln began by citing facts from his lawyer's brief. Twenty-three of the thirty-nine framers of the Constitution had voted for the slave-free Northwest Ordinance, he said, a clear implication that the founding fathers believed Congress should control slavery in the territories. This contradicted the Supreme Court's Dred Scott decision.[25] Lincoln argued that the Republican party did not stand for sectionalism - they were conservatives, not radical revolutionaries. He spoke to the south, pleading for better understanding, explaining that John Brown, who had recently focused the nation's attention on Harpers Ferry,[26] was not a Republican, and that no Republican either aided or abetted him.[27]

The audience soon grasped the strength of Lincoln's argument and the reasoning behind the prairie lawyer's logic. Interrupted several times by applause, Lincoln closed with the memorable phrase, "Let us have faith that right makes might, and in that faith let us to the end dare to do our duty as we understand it." [28]

Cheers, applause, and a standing ovation followed Lincoln's final statement. The <u>Tribune</u>, reporting that no political figure had ever made such a favorable first impression, printed and distributed his speech throughout the country. Lincoln had calculated correctly; the Cooper Union talk had made him a national figure, capable of winning a presidential nomination. Although many Republicans came away convinced that they had indeed found the right man to nominate for president, Lincoln remained modest. He wrote to his wife, "The speech at New-York, being within my calculation before I started, went off passing well, and gave me no trouble whatsoever."[29]

Lincoln did win the nomination and the election of 1860 which prompted southern states to secede, bringing on the Civil War. During the first few years of the conflict Henry Ward Beecher raised money for equipping local regiments and spoke endlessly on patriotic themes. In the process he wore himself out and in the fall of 1863 he decided to take a "rest" trip and travel to England to relax.[30]

Shut off from its main supply of cotton, Great Britain had suffered severe unemployment in its textile industry. This created great hostility to President Lincoln's government, and Beecher decided to make several speeches in England to strengthen the federal cause and to counteract southern propaganda. He received chilly receptions in Liverpool and Manchester, hotbeds of Confederate sympathizers. Although Beecher may not have swayed all of his listeners, he did impress them. One newspaper reported that "Mr. Beecher's audacity in lecturing at all had a trace of sublimity in it." Hostile audiences held anti-Beecher placards, quoting him as saying in 1861, during the Trent Affair,[31] "the best blood of England must flow for the outrage England had perpetrated on America," and they jeered and heckled him. He wrote to his friend Theodore Tilton, however, that he felt some sort of "out-of-body sensation" while delivering his talks, never fearing the threats he heard or read about."I have a perverse and ludicrous sympathy with the rascals," he confessed, "If I could only establish a duality and keep one self speaking I think with the other I would go down into the crowd and tell them how to point their mischief a good deal more wittily and efficiently." And he wrote to his brother Charles, "In spite of their faults I like the English. Put that in your pipe and smoke it."[32]

Beecher returned home feeling that he had helped America's beleaguered friends in England by supporting their anti-slavery convictions. He had used his skills to defend his country and its goals. Feted at the Brooklyn Academy of Music and at his church, he continued to speak out for President Lincoln's policies, campaigned for Lincoln's re-election in 1864, and became the president's choice for the main speaker during the flag-restoring ceremonies at Fort Sumter, South Carolina, after the fort's recovery by Union forces in 1865.[33]

In post-war years Beecher campaigned for women's rights, temperance, and Jewish-Christian relationships. After a highly publicized adultery trial in 1875, he lost some of his long time glitter, even though he was exonerated. He died on March 3, 1887, at 124 Hicks Street, and was buried in Green-Wood Cemetery.[34]

[1] Brooklyn Almanac, p.65.
Brooklyn City Directory, 1861.

[2] Hoogenboom, Olive, The History of the First Unitarian Church of Brooklyn Heights (Brooklyn, 1987), p.53.

[3] Centennial At St. Patrick's Church, Brooklyn 1849-1949, pamphlet, N.Y.P.L.

One Hundredth Anniversary of the R.C.Diocese of Brooklyn, 1853-1953, published by the Tablet, vol. XLVl, no. 37.

[4] Black Churches in Brooklyn, pamphlet, B.H.S., 1984.
Weeksville, Then and Now.

[5] Centennial at St. Patrick's Church, Brooklyn, 1849-1949, pamphlet.
One Hundredth Anniversary of the R.C. Diocese of Brooklyn, 1853-1953.
Brooklyn Almanac, p.30.

[6] Henry, Stuart C., Unvanquished Puritan, A Portrait of Lyman Beecher(Grand Rapids, 1973), p.291,292.

[7] Hibbin, Paxton, Henry Ward Beecher An American Portrait(N.Y., 1927), pp.98,107.
Duduit, James M., Henry Ward Beecher and the Political Pulpit, doctoral dissertation, Florida State University, 1983, pp.20,56.

[8] Henry Ward Beecher An American Portrait, p.98.
Reminiscences of Brooklyn, lecture by Horatio King, March 7, 1891.

[9] Brooklyn Era, January 11, 1862.

[10] New York A Guide to the Metropolis, p.300.

[11] The Civil War Dictionary, pp.69, 448.

[12] Henry Ward Beecher and the Political Pulpit, p.86.

[13] Brooklyn Eagle, June 1,1856.

[14] Ibid.

[15] Beecher Family Papers, B.H.S.

[16] Ibid.

[17] Brooklyn Eagle, May 27, 1927.

[18] Mr. Lincoln Goes To New York, p.36.

[19] Mr. Lincoln Goes To New York, p.37.

Braden, Waldo W., Abraham Lincoln, Public Speaker(Baton Rouge, 1988),p.33.

Herndon's Lincoln, American Historical Landmarks, edited by David F. Hawke(Indianapolis, 1970),pp.194-197.

Thomas, Benjamin, Abraham Lincoln, A Biography(N.Y., 1952), pp.201-204.

[20] Mr. Lincoln Goes To New York, p.38.

Abraham Lincoln, A Biography, pp. 201,202,204.

[21] Herndon's Lincoln, pp.195-197.

[22] New York Times, February 25, 1860.

Abraham Lincoln,A Biography, pp.202-204.

[23] Brochure, Plymouth Church.

New York, A Guide to the Metropolis, p.356.

Brooklyn is America, p.70.

[24] Mr. Lincoln Goes to New York, p.85.

[25] The 1857 Dred Scott decision rendered the Missouri Compromise, which had prohibited slavery in the Wisconsin Territory, where Scott had lived, unconstitutional.

[26] John Brown, a fanatical abolitionist, took possesion of the Harpers Ferry, Virginia, armory, as a first step in his plan to free southern slaves.

[27] Abraham Lincoln, A Biography, p.202.

Mr. Lincoln Goes to New York, p.85.

The Life and Writings of Abraham Lincoln, edited by Philip Van Doren Stern, New York, 1940, p.569.

[28] Cooper Union speech, February 27, 1860.

The Life and Writings of Abraham Lincoln, pp.569,571,572,580,581.

[29] Oates, Stephen P., With Malice Toward None(N.Y., 1977),

p.173,174.

The Life and Writings of Abraham Lincoln, p.569.

Abraham Lincoln, A Biography, p.204.

[30] Beecher family papers, B.H.S.

[31] In November, 1861, the United States warship, San Jacinto, stopped the British mail ship Trent off the coast of Cuba, and took from the vessel Confederate envoys John Slidell and James M. Mason. This diplomatic incident, the most serious of the Civil War, almost caused hostilities to break out between England and America.

[32] Beecher family papers, Yale Univerity Library.

The British Tour of Henry Ward Beecher, Edward Ellsworth, The Lincoln Herald, 1971, pp.138-149.

[33] Ostrander, Stephen M.,A History of the City of Brooklyn (Brooklyn, 1894), 2 Vol., Vol.2, p.125.

[34] New York Times, March 9, 1887.

Unvanquished Puritan, p.292.

The Boroughs of Brooklyn and Queens, Counties of Nassau and Suffolk, Long Island, N.Y. 1609-1924, edited by Henry Isham Hazelton, New York, 1925, 7 vol., vol.3, p.1315.

WALT WHITMAN

America's Civil War made a deep and lasting impression on Walt Whitman. Although his masterpiece, <u>Leaves of Grass</u> was published in 1855, some of his best writing, including <u>Drum Taps</u> and <u>O Captain, My Captain</u>, had their genesis in Whitman's wartime experience. Whitman even considered <u>Drum-Taps</u> superior to <u>Leaves of Grass</u> because it could "express in a poem...the pending action of this time and land we swim in."[1]

Some critics regard Whitman as the "father of free verse," and America's most influential writer. The poet somehow reached an intimacy with readers that others failed to achieve, and this accomplishment secured him a special niche in the pantheon of American literary gods. More than fifty books have been written attempting to describe both Whitman and his writings, and when the New York City Public Library held a Walt Whitman exhibit in 1925 they filled forty cases with manuscripts, photos, and miscellanea. Some critics consider his <u>Leaves of Grass</u> one of the greatest books ever written, placing its author in a class with Shakespeare and Homer. Others denigrated his work for its <u>avant garde</u> form insisting that he repelled as many readers as he attracted. In his obituary, the New York <u>Times</u> said that they could not call him a great poet, but they did give him credit for having "flashes of something occasionally like genius expressed in something occasionally like English."[2]

Whitman's father, an itinerant carpenter, moved his growing family from Huntington in Suffolk County, New

York, to the village of Brooklyn in 1823. He would buy a house, enhance its appearance, sell it, and move to another, so the Whitmans lived in a succession of homes on Front, Cranberry, Johnson, Adams, Tillary and Henry streets. By 1835 there were eight children: Jesse, the oldest, then Walt, now twelve, sisters Mary and Hannah Louise, brothers Andrew, George Washington, Thomas Jefferson (Jeff), and Edward.[3]

Brooklyn's best-known citizen, dubbed the "good grey poet" by his friend, William O'Connor, began his writing career at age eleven, with "sentimental bits" printed by the Long Island Patriot and the New York Mirror. He practiced the printer's trade briefly, but in 1836 returned to Long Island to teach school in East Norwich, Hempstead, Babylon, Long Swamp, and Smithtown. At 23 he began writing and editing for the New York Aurora, the Evening Tattler, and the Long Island Star. From 1846 until 1848 he had a "pleasant sit" as editor of the Brooklyn Eagle, ending his tenure there because of political disagreements with owner Isaac Van Anden. He then travelled south with his younger brother Jeff, and wrote for the New Orleans Crescent from March until May 1848. Tiring of Dixie, and perhaps a tad homesick, he returned to Brooklyn via the Mississippi River, the Great Lakes, and the Hudson River. Back in Brooklyn, Whitman operated a printing office and ran a stationery store. In 1855 the Rome Brothers of Brooklyn Heights published his Leaves of Grass. While living with his family at 107 North Portland Street, he edited the Brooklyn Times and referred to himself in the Brooklyn city directory as a copyist.[4]

At the start of the Civil War in April 1861, Whitman worked for the Brooklyn Standard (Fulton and Pineapple streets), contributing twenty-five articles on the past and present of his hometown, calling it <u>Brooklyniana</u>. He described old families, Revolutionary War prison ships, eighteenth century churches and their burial grounds, the fire department, and entertainment.[5]

Whitman also spent a good deal of his time writing poems and articles for the Boston <u>Evening Transcript</u>, the New York <u>Leader</u>, and <u>Harpers Weekly</u>, and reading his work aloud in Pfaff's Cave, his favorite tavern, on New York's Broadway. He frequently spent the evening there deep in conversation, often arguing in defense of the Union. The <u>Leader</u> articles described his first contact with sick and wounded soldiers at the Broadway Hospital, located near Pearl Street in New York. He described the patients, their ailments, and the doctors, offering a realistic look at daily hospital routines, including details of several "fine operations."[6]

Whitman loved ordinary people and the theater, writing frequently on both subjects. None of his work, however, bore the Whitman name, as he wrote under the banner "Velsor Brush," a pseudonym created from his mother's and grandmother's maiden names (Van Velsor and Brush). From his writing and copying he earned a comfortable living of from six dollars to seven dollars a week.[7]

Whitman's fondness for the stage took him to Mary Provost's theater where he saw the great Junius Booth's son, J. Wilkes, play <u>Richard III</u>. Although the young Booth received favorable notices from the press he did not impress Whitman, who scornfully thought that comparing Wilkes' performance with that of his father was like comparing a bust of Henry

Clay with the great orator himself.[8]

Whitman's brother George, who had enlisted for a three-month period as an officer in the Fifty-first New York Volunteers, sustained a wound during the battle of Fredericksburg. Upon seeing an item in the New York Herald listing a Lieutenant "Whitmore" among the casualties the poet hastened to Washington to ascertain the seriousness of George's injury. Whitman arrived there dead broke after being robbed while changing trains in Philadelphia. Borrowing money from old friend William O'Connor, Whitman persuaded another acquaintance, Charles Eldridge, to obtain a pass for him to visit Falmouth, Virginia, the site of George's outfit. Fearing the worst, he was greatly relieved to find George recuperating nicely, suffering only slight inconvenience from a minor facial wound.[9]

Whitman spent a few days with his brother, experiencing first-hand the horrors of army hospitals and their daily amputations, before returning to Washington with a boatload of injured soldiers. While chatting with them and offering succor, Whitman realized what comfort his ministrations could provide. He decided to stay on, becoming a "soldier's missionary" to sick and wounded servicemen, a nineteenth century one-man U.S.O troupe.[10] Whitman secured a position in the paymaster's office and took lodgings at William O'Connor's home, sharing the family's meals. Connected with no organized agency Whitman began visiting sick and wounded soldiers on a regular basis. He spent hours preparing for a hospital visit in order to "exude the perfection of physical health and to present as cheerful an appearance as possible." He frequently arrived with oranges, apples, spiced fruit, pickles, small containers of jelly, or plugs of tobacco to distribute. He handed out combs, toothbrushes, undershirts, stockings, writing paper, pens, envelopes, pencils, and reading material. But mainly he acted as a friend and surrogate family to ailing, lonely, often despondent men who otherwise saw no visitors. "Friendship could cure a fever and daily affection a bad wound," he said, and he believed that he saved more than one life with his warmth and concern.[11]

Whitman's younger brother Jeff worked at the Brooklyn Water Works as a hydraulic engineer.[12] They corresponded frequently and argued about the merits of Confederate general Robert E. Lee, Union general Joseph Hooker, and the battle of Chancellorsville. Very opinionated, Jeff had no love for President Lincoln, believing him not up to the task, and he held the Irish responsible for the New York Draft Riots of July 1863, writing, "Walt, I am perfectly rabid on an Irishman."[13]

Jeff earned ninety dollars per month and sometimes more when he ran surveys in upstate New York and Massachusetts. His attitude on the administration notwithstanding, Jeff and his fellow engineers aided Walt's good work in Washington by channelling a steady stream of money to him, so much so that his compatriots referred to themselves as the Brooklyn Water Works Soldier's Aid Society. Walt received from six to seven dollars weekly from both the engineers and others, including Moses Lane, the chief engineer, and Isaac Van Anden, his former employer at the Brooklyn Eagle.[14]

Despite his long hours of hospital work, Whitman read avidly, including the Bible, Dante's Inferno, and the works of Virgil. He described himself, "as much of a beauty as ever or more so - weigh about two hundred and beard and neck are terrible to behold, with so much hair like a great wild buffalo." In late June 1864 he became a victim himself, experiencing spells of faintness and terrible head and throat pains. Ordered to stay home, Whitman returned to Brooklyn where he suffered severely for several weeks, not even venturing outside until mid-July. He described his illness as "tenacious, peculiar and baffling" and only a sudden "current change" allayed his fears of being in for a very long siege. He rallied very quickly, however, and soon began riding, sailing, and spending time at the seashore near Coney Island. By September he had recovered completely and began to visit the Brooklyn City Hospital on Raymond Street, a quarter mile from his house. In 1862 he had reported that this edifice had "a noble appearance and was kept scrupulously clean and neat." Two years later, suffering from an overcrowding of wounded patients, it had changed. Whitman now found it "a bad place, one that lacked cleanliness, proper nursing facilities and that served only rice and molasses for Sunday dinner." He felt the old urge to visit, knowing that days would elapse without the wounded or sick ever having a visitor. He wrote to a friend, Mrs. D. Nelly O'Connor," I am still in business."[15]

Always the political animal, Whitman attended rallies and lamented the ubiquitous presence of the Copperheads who opposed President Lincoln's wartime policies and called for peace at any price. He wrote to Nelly's husband William that he was disenchanted with Brooklyn, believing that ninety per cent of the people he saw wore McClellan buttons, announcing their support of former army commander General George B.

McClellan, who ran against Abraham Lincoln in the 1864 presidential election. The rallies sometimes drew fifteen thousand to twenty thousand people who saw fireworks, clusters of gas lights, countless torches, and banners.[16]

In a newspaper article Whitman wrote about the Fifty-first New York Volunteers and a certain Captain G. Whitman. This unsigned item bore the poet's touch. He singled out Brooklyn soldiers, especially his brother, and related anecdotes concerning them, citing the dangers, fatigue, and hardships they endured. He brought the war closer to home by mentioning the Brooklynites he met: Frederick B. McReady, Amos Vliet, Charley Parker, John Lowry, Allen V. King, Michael Lally, and Patrick Hennessy.[17]

In January 1865 Whitman's brother George, back in action with the Ninth Corps, was captured and confined in Danville, Virginia. George's trunk arrived the day after Christmas, having been forwarded by a friend, Lieutenant Babcock. The family felt ill at ease by its presence and procrastinated several days before opening it. They found trousers, coats, a sash, a revolver, and a diary. Included, too, were photographs of men, several of whom had been killed in action. Whitman read George's diary, proclaiming it "a perfect poem of the war." On February 24 they received a note from him. He had just arrived in Annapolis, Maryland, after being exchanged and would soon be returning home.[18]

In January 1865 while working at the Department of Interior, Whitman wrote a lengthy article for the Brooklyn <u>Daily Union</u>, detailing his brother's experiences. Whitman calculated that George had travelled some twenty thousand miles in four years and had fought under Generals Irvin

McDowell, George B. McLellan, Ambrose Burnside, John Pope, George Meade, William Sherman, and Ulysses S. Grant.[19]

While home for an Easter visit, Whitman learned that President Abraham Lincoln, with whom he had a nodding acquaintance, had been assassinated. Absolutely shocked, the entire family could do nothing more than read all the local newspapers and pass them from person to person silently. The following day Whitman took a ferry to New York, walked the silent streets, and noted the absence of the city's normal bustle and enthusiasm. Broadway, he said, looked like one huge funeral parlor, with its doors shuttered and black fringed flags at half mast.[20]

After the war Whitman revised Leaves of Grass continually, eventually accounting for nine editions. Specimen Days, published in 1882 presented not only his Civil War experience but also his views of America during the nineteenth century. Paralyzed by a stroke in 1873, Whitman never recovered completely. He lived with his brother George, a city inspector, in Camden, New Jersey, and died there on March 26, 1892.[21]

[1] Carpenter, George R., Walt Whitman(New York,1909), p.99.
[2] New York Times, March 27, 1892.
    Allen, Gay Wilson, The Solitary Singer(N.Y.,1967), preface, p.ix.
    Holloway, Emory, Whitman(New York,1969),preface, p.ix.
[3] The Solitary Singer, pp.2,5.
    Walt Whitman, A Life, p.65.
[4] Brooklyn City Directory, 1860.

The Solitary Singer, pp.23,26,27,45,54,73,90-92.

Dear Brother Walt, edited by Dennis Berthold and Kenneth M. Price, Kent, Ohio, 1984, p.xvi.

Walt Whitman, A Life(New York,1980), p.306.

[5] Brooklyn Standard, June 3, 1861.

The Solitary Singer, p.276.

[6] The Solitary Singer, p.277,278.

Walt Whitman, A Life, p.263.

Starr, Louis M., The Bohemian Brigade(N.Y., 1954), p.4.

[7] Walt Whitman and the Civil War, edited by Charles I. Glicksberg, N.Y., 1933, pp.17,21.

[8] Walt Whitman and the Civil War, p.56.

[9] The Solitary Singer, pp.281,283.

Walt Whitman A Life, p.268.

Dear Brother Walt, p.18.

[10] The United Service Organizations (U.S.O.) of World War II fame specialized in entertaining servicemen, both at home and abroad.

The Solitary Singer, p.286.

[11] Brooklyn Eagle, March 19,1863.

The Solitary Singer, pp.286,288-290.

Dear Brother Walt, p.42.

[12] He would one day gain fame as an outstanding hydraulic engineer and superintendent of the St. Louis, Missouri, water works.

[13] Dear Brother Walt, p.66.

Walt Whitman A Life, p.293.

The Solitary Singer, p.306.

[14] Dear Brother Walt, pp.xxiii,xxiv,44,45.

The Solitary Singer, p.290.

[15] Letter to Nelly O'Connor, September 11,1864, the Berg Collection, New York Public Library.

Letter to George Eldridge, July 9,1864

Letter to Lewis K. Browne, July 11,1864.

Walt Whitman's Civil War, edited by Walter Lowenfels, New York, 1960, p.105.

The Solitary Singer, pp.295.

Walt Whitman A Life, pp.293,294,296.

Walt Whitman's New York, edited by Henry M. Christman, N.Y.,1963, pp.132,133.

Walt Whitman and the Civil War, p.169.

[16] Letter to Charles Eldridge, October 8,1864.

Letter to William D. O'Connor, September 11,1864.

The Solitary Singer, p.316.

[17] New York Times, October 29,1864.

[18] Letters to William O'Connor, January 20,1865, March 26,1865, April 7,1865.

Walt Whitman A Life, p.297,298.

Marinacci, Barbara, O Wondrous Singer(Cornwall, N.Y.,1970), pp.230,232.

The Solitary Singer, p.330.

[19] The Solitary Singer, p.317.

Walt Whitman's Civil War, pp.86-89.

[20] Walt Whitman and the Civil War, p.174.

Walt Whitman A Life, p.302.

[21] New York Times, March 26,1892.

Whitman, Walt, Leaves of Grass, introduction by Gay Wilson Allen, N.Y., 1958.

THE NEWSPAPERS

During the 1860s Brooklyn's newspapers offered a variety of opinions on President Lincoln and the Civil War. The <u>Eagle</u> and the <u>Standard</u>, the best of that era, exhibited chagrin at Lincoln's victory in the presidential election of 1860, and the <u>Eagle</u> proved very slow in adapting to the change from peace to war, causing immense problems for itself.[1]

The <u>Eagle</u> began life as the Brooklyn <u>Eagle and Kings County Democrat</u> in October 1841, predating Henry Raymond's New York <u>Times</u> by a decade. It lasted until March 17, 1955, when it sold its machinery at auction and closed its doors forever. In painful irony, it had endured for one hundred fourteen years and then collapsed just seven months before its beloved "Bums," the Brooklyn Dodgers, finally subdued their hated rivals, the New York Yankees, in the baseball World Series.[2]

Henry C. Murphy, an extraordinarily accomplished Brooklynite, whose career included terms as mayor, congressman, state senator, and minister to the Netherlands, founded the paper. Walt Whitman edited it from 1845 until 1848 but his successor, Samuel G. Arnold, modernized it, truncating its name in 1850 and adding steam power to its press a year later. Arnold's enthusiasm for preacher Henry Ward Beecher's anti-slavery rhetoric, however, ran counter to the politics of owner Isaac Van Anden, and so in 1853 Arnold resigned in favor of Henry McCloskey, a Breckinridge Democrat.[3] The new editor's bitter wartime editorials would one day bring charges of disloyalty upon the paper.[4]

The Eagle did not favor Abraham Lincoln in the election of 1860, and with great pain announced on November 7 that it "would bow to the majestic decision of the people rendered in accordance with the forms of the Constitution." Most Brooklyn papers echoed this same theme.[5]

As the president-elect prepared for his inauguration the Eagle concentrated on the imminent war and Beecher's sermons on it, Brooklyn's first opera, and the city's self-image. The paper, a four-page six-column journal, sold for two cents. In 1860, page one, except for literary news, featured advertisements, theater schedules, medical advertisements, and rental notices. After the Confederate attack on Fort Sumter, however, war news appeared and soon dominated the front page. Editorials and foreign news appeared on page two, along with more ads and a report of the Board of Aldermen's and Supervisor's meeting. Page three gave local news, play reviews, European news, and gossip, while page four had business notices and installments of a novel. The paper had the highest circulation of any evening paper in the nation.[6]

Feeling lukewarm about the war, the Eagle accused the government of driving the southern states out of the Union. It also warned of internecine warfare and military despotism. These opinions made the Eagle's support for the war effort seem tepid, and on the night of April 17, a hostile mob of several hundred "patriots" roamed the streets to confront the paper. They visited 30 Fulton Street in a fury. "Show your colors, hang out your flag," they demanded, and tried to force their way in. The night watchman waved the flag, and the mob, satisfied with its triumph, turned to other "less than patriotic" newspapers, the News (368 Fulton Street), the Standard

(Pineapple and Fulton Streets), and the Star (104 Orange Street).[7]

As McCloskey's strident editorials questioned the government's wisdom, a federal grand jury met on August 16, 1861, to inquire whether five New York City area newspapers, including the Brooklyn Daily and Weekly Eagle were not guilty of disloyalty by suggesting that the south's demands should be met. McCloskey responded boldly that the government obviously spoke in ignorance - a weekly Eagle had not been published in seven years. He added that the paper would vindicate and maintain the principle of free speech and in a rather familiar flourish added, "if this be treason they can make the most of it."[8]

No indictments followed, but Postmaster Horatio King ordered his Brooklyn counterpart, George B. Lincoln, to suspend the Eagle's mailing privileges, a severe measure. Defiance notwithstanding, Henry McCloskey resigned, to be replaced by Thomas Kinsella. The next day the government removed the "disabilities" imposed on the the paper.[9]

Two Eagle employees perpetrated one of the Civil War's most elaborate hoaxes. In May 1864 they forged an official presidential proclamation calling for an additional draft of four hundred thousand men and a national day of fasting. Such foreboding usually sent the price of gold skyrocketing, exactly what the con men had in mind. By using the names of Abraham Lincoln and Secretary of State William H. Seward on the bottom of imitation Associated Press paper, they created enough verisimilitude to fool many of New York's major newspapers. Lorenzo Croewse, night editor of the New York Times, however, smelled a rat. He did not recognize the handwriting and suspected that such an important announcement would not have come from a novice. In checking, he discovered that the Herald never received the original and that the Associated Press considered it a fraud. The Daily News stopped its production run, and the Herald destroyed twenty thousand copies that had already been printed. The World and the Journal of Commerce, however, both anti-administration newspapers, decided to go ahead with their "extra."[10]

This "news" strained even Abraham Lincoln's famous forbearance, and the angry president ordered Secretary of State Seward to have Major General John Dix, commander of the New York department, halt the malefactor's presses and arrest their owners. Dix, feeling that the papers were genuinely duped, hesitated to make the arrests, but he did shut down both newspapers.[11]

The police took an Eagle reporter, Joseph Howard, Jr., in for questioning as he had been bragging that the price of gold would suddenly soar. Under pressure Howard blurted out the truth, and he and a cohort, Francis Mallison, received jail sentences at the Fort Lafayette prison. Mallison gained a pardon from President Lincoln after intercession by the young man's ailing mother, but Howard languished in jail for two months until his father, an influential parishioner in Henry Ward Beecher's church, pleaded with the minister to use his influence to gain his son's freedom. Between Beecher's importuning and Lincoln's lack of vindictiveness, Howard obtained his release.[12]

The incident, many said, showed that the government always overreacted, and New York Governor Horatio Seymour attempted to have General Dix indicted for making illegal seizures. These efforts failed, but the anti-administration newspapers had a field day criticizing Washington for interfering with "freedom of the press."[13]

Some of the city's newspapers provided articles more theatrical than newsworthy. The <u>Standard</u> ran the following under "Important From Washington": "The city is to be evacuated by the Lincoln administration and the government archives removed north. J. Davis contemplates permanent residence in the federal capital. Government buildings are to be blown up. It is also a fact that on Monday of this week by order of Davis, his agent not only hired a pew in the Unitarian Church in Washington City but on Tuesday a fine silver plate with the name of Jefferson Davis engraved hereon was placed on the pew door."[14]

The <u>Standard</u>, too, had opposed Lincoln's candidacy, and on hearing of the Republican victory in 1860, the paper agreed to "reluctantly bow in submission as all America should to the popular will." The paper, however, reminded its readers "that whenever Mr. Lincoln is right we shall so express ourselves and when we disagree we shall say so as we have always done, boldly and fearlessly." Indeed, the <u>Standard</u> had as its motto "Truth Without Fear." The paper believed that Lincoln, without a working majority in the House and Senate, could not carry into effect any of the doctrines he espoused, the ones that had caused the country so much excitement. And this might have been true had the southern states not seceded.[15]

Despite occasional criticism, the <u>Standard</u> generally supported the government and regularly chided the <u>Herald</u>, the <u>News</u>, and the <u>Eagle</u> for their overt hostility toward the administration. The paper's support for the war was not just talk; on October 11, 1862, owner and former alderman, James R. Del Vecchio, enlisted in the Union army and led part of the Empire Brigade in combat.[16]

Other papers came and went. B. Spooner and Son published the Evening Star and the Weekly Star. A fickle Democratic party deprived them of municipal patronage, and the paper ceased publication in June 1863. The City News, owned by W.G. Bishop and S.W. Morton, came out weekly. It could have supplanted the Eagle as Brooklyn's most esteemed paper during the Eagle's "troubles," but its management apparently could not cut the mustard. It consolidated with the Daily Union (10 Front Street) in November 1863. The Era, an eight-page literary journal, proved unsuccessful and shifted to New York, where it became the New York Era. Other papers included George C. Bennett's Daily Times (12 South 7th Street) and the German language Long Island Anzeiger, edited by Henry E. Roehr. Der Apologet (the Apology), a German language weekly, ran from June 1861 to February 1862, and the Williamsburg Journal, a weekly literary/political paper, edited by J. Douglass Robinson, of 144 Grand Street in the Eastern District, appeared for a few months in 1861. In addition, the New York Times ran a special Brooklyn column several times a week.[17]

[1] The Eagle and Brooklyn, p.11.

[2] The Eagle and Brooklyn, pp.3,19,23.

[3] A pro-slavery Kentuckian, John C. Breckinridge served as vice president in President James Buchanan's administration and ran against Abraham Lincoln in the presidential

election of 1860.

[4] The City of Brooklyn A Political History, p.21.
Brooklyn Almanac, p.31.
The Eagle and Brooklyn, pp.29,30,59,60.

[5] The Eagle and Brooklyn, pp.11.

[6] Brooklyn Eagle, March 6,1861.
The Eagle and Brooklyn, pp.59.

[7] The Eagle and Brooklyn, p.64.
A History of the City of Brooklyn,(Ostrander), vol.2, p.118.
Brooklyn Eagle, April 13,1861.

[8] Brooklyn Eagle, August 8,1861.
The Eagle and Brooklyn, pp.64-65.

[9] The City of Brooklyn A Political History, p.21.
The Eagle and Brooklyn, p.65.
Brooklyn Eagle, September 7,1861.

[10] Trudeau, Noel, Bloody Roads South(N.Y., 1989), pp.194,195.
The Great Civil War Gold Hoax, Jeffrey D. Wert, American
History Illustrated, April,1980, Vol.xv, No. 1, pp.20-24.
The History of the City of Brooklyn(Stiles), vol.2, p.472.
The Eagle and Brooklyn, p.65.

[11] The Great Civil War Gold Hoax, pp.20-24.
Bloody Road South, pp.194,195.
Brandt, Nat, The Man Who Tried to Burn New
York(Syracuse, 1986), p.208.
A History of the City of Brooklyn,(Stiles),p.472.

[12] Unvanquished Puritan, p.159.
The Great Civil War Gold Hoax, pp.20-24.

[13] The Great Civil War Hoax, pp.20-24.
The Eagle and Brooklyn, p.65

[14] Brooklyn Standard, April 13,1861.

[15] Brooklyn <u>Standard</u>, October 11,1862.

[16] <u>Ibid</u>., October 11,1862

[17] Brooklyn <u>Era</u>, December 21,1861.

<u>The History of the City of Brooklyn</u>,(Stiles) Vol.3, pp.927-943.

<u>A History of the City of Brooklyn</u>,(Ostrander), vol.2, p.128.

ENTERTAINMENT

The city's entertainment industry thrived during the Civil War. Brooklynites flocked to theaters, minstrel shows, and lecture halls in order to relax and get away from the newspaper's daily fare of battles and casualty lists. Soldiers home on furlough attended many of these morale-boosting diversions and just the appearance of a man in uniform often resulted in the singing of patriotic songs, including the <u>Star Spangled Banner</u>, which was growing in popularity. The Mecca of Brooklyn's top-quality entertainment was its Academy of Music.

In 1858, a group of prominent citizens, including the Pierreponts, Brevoorts, Lows, and Sands, proposed the construction of a building for the presentation of "innocent and instructive amusements." Three years later, shortly before the Civil War began, the original Brooklyn Academy of Music rose on Montague Street between Clinton and Court amidst much publicity. It cost three hundred thousand dollars, but the response to public subscription proved so successful that it opened debt free. In apparent deference to its religious members, the board of directors hired a church architect. He created a cathedral-like twenty-three hundred-seat theater with a magnificent stage suitable for large scale opera, drama, or concert. Reserved balcony or parquet seats sold for one dollar, regular balcony seats for fifty cents, and family circle seats for twenty-five cents.[1]

On opening day, January 15, 1861, a capacity audience heard Madame Pauline Colson and the well-known Italians, Pasquale Brignoli, Nicola Ferri, and Fillippo Coletti sing solos and duets from the works of Mozart, Verdi, and Donizetti. The Academy's first opera opened on January 22, with Il Guiramento substituted for La Traviata at the last moment. Religious pressures prevented the performance of a work in which the heroine had questionable morals. Mary Todd Lincoln, the president-elect's wife, in New York for inaugural shopping, attended with two of her sons.[2]

Since many citizens still viewed certain entertainment as "the devil's work," the Academy banned drama for its first eleven months, barring both Edwin Booth and James H. Hackett, the foremost actors of the day. But with the press, especially the Eagle, pushing for more contemporary theater, the directors finally succumbed to the public's demands and on December 23, 1861, E.L. Davenport and Julia Bennett Barrow starred in Shakespeare's Hamlet, receiving excellent reviews. Edwin Forrest appeared in November 1862 in Virginius, Hamlet, and Richelieu, and by invitation of the mayor and leading citizens, Edwin Booth starred in Richelieu on December 23rd. Laura Keene [3] played in She Stoops to Conquer on January 14, 1863, and Lucille Watson, Matilda Huron, and Miss Keene all appeared from April 28 through May 9, 1863, in a series of plays including Don Caesar De Bazan, The Loan of a Lover, Lucrezia Borgia, and Perfection. Within the space of two weeks Brooklyn enjoyed the performances of three of America's most talented actresses.[4]

In the Fall of 1863, the actor John Wilkes Booth, who would assassinate President Abraham Lincoln less than two years hence, played at the Academy of Music. On October 24, 1863, the Eagle ran the following advertisement:

J. Wilkes Booth's first night in Brooklyn with Mrs.

Julia Barrett Barrow. Mr. Booth begs to announce that he will make his first appearance as the Duke of Gloster in Shakespeare's tragedy Richard III.[5]

Two days later Booth starred as Phidias and Raphel in Marble Heart, also with Mrs. Barrow. In these, his only appearances in Brooklyn, he received mixed notices, as indicated in this excerpt from one local review.[6]

"The Booth and Barrow combination.

"J. Wilkes Booth made his first appearance in Brooklyn last Saturday evening at the Academy of Music in Richard III. Mr. Booth has the advantage of a recommendation to favor through an illustrious name and the disadvantage of inevitable comparison with his father, and his brother, Edwin. The latter he strongly resembles in feature, physique and quality of voice, but he is inferior in several important particulars. His performance lacks the grace, finish and repose of Edwin; his enunciation is indistinct and he betrays at times a tendency to rant. There, are, however, flashes of real power. I was particularly and favorably impressed with the scene of the killing of Henry and with the whole of the fourth act. The difficult wooing scene did not please me so well. The 'terrific broadsword combat' as it was sensationally described on the bills, was intensely gratifying to the gallery, Mr. Booth fencing well and introducing some new and effective business."[7]

The Academy also saw important political and public gatherings, many of which exerted considerable influence in forming public opinion. On October 7, 1862, a large crowd assembled to endorse President Lincoln's Emancipation Proclamation, and a great Union rally was held there on March 16, 1863. From then until 1903, when the building burned down, nearly every presidential candidate spoke at the Brooklyn Academy of Music.[8]

In September 1863 Gabriel Harrison opened his Park Theater on Fulton Street, providing competition for the Academy which some felt had become too expensive and elitist. Named after the famous old New York City playhouse, it presented a "brilliant array of the beauty and fashion of Brooklyn" to a standing-room audience, and followed that with A Married Life and A Loan of a Lover, starring Miss Henrietta Irving and Mary Shaw. Walter Lennox Low also performed as a "low" comedian who was "funny without being vulgar."[9]

Other forms of entertainment, besides the theater, thrived. In October 1861 Lent's Great National Circus, featuring Joe Pentland, the clown, opened at Fulton Street and DeKalb Avenue while the Bohemian Glass Blower performed at the Musical Hall at Fulton and Orange Streets. The Winter Garden, a "saloon of music and recreation," held concerts every Monday and Thursday nights and at the Cremona on Myrtle Avenue the three Dobson Brothers, billed as the "greatest banjoists in the world," played three evenings a week. On December 22, just in time for the holidays, a new arena opened on Raymond Street between Fulton Street and De Kalb Avenue. It featured a troupe of equestriennes, all attractive and talented enough to make the enterprise a success. Burtis' Varieties, at Fulton and Pineapple Streets, featured Kate Waters, the "charming danseuse and comedienne"; William B. Harrison, the great extemporaneous poet; Eph Burgess, the "unrivalled" jig dancer; M. West, the Ethiopian Delineator; and Harry Pell, the great stump orator.

In September 1862 Hooley's Opera House opened at Court and Remsen streets and became Brooklyn's first permanent company. It featured the Hooley Minstrels along with Master Eddie, a female impersonator.[10]

Charles F. Brown (Artemus Ward), the "funniest writer in the country," lectured at the Aetheneum and after an absence of many years, the original General Tom Thumb[11] appeared at the Brooklyn Institute on Washington Street. His show included "good singing, instrumental music and the services of competent artists." Admission to see the "Lilliputian General" was fifteen cents for adults and ten cents for children.[12]

During the winter of 1862 an ice-skating mania swept Brooklyn. Participants used the Washington, Nassau, and Willow ponds near 3rd Avenue and 48th Street, the Chichester in Bushwick, and the Monitor in Greenpoint. They skated at the Capitoline on Nostrand Avenue, the Poplar Pond near 9th Avenue and 4th Street, and Dumbleton's Pond, not far from the base ball grounds on Myrtle Avenue. The famous Union Pond advertised a pagoda "brilliantly illuminated" by the famous pyrotechnist Mr. Hatfield, and it also featured a parade, an ice carnival, and a band. The "strictest police regulations" insured order at all times.[13]

The Era admonished young ladies to skate frequently as it would give them strength, energy, and beauty while developing their forms and planting "roses and carnations" upon their cheeks. In addition it would lengthen their lives as the exercise would expand the chest, strengthen the hips, and invigorate the entire system. Better skaters would mean better mothers, they added, as children born of puny women would cause the race to degenerate mentally and physically.[14]

During the intense heat of the summer many Brooklynites took advantage of the city's shoreline and bathed in its surrounding waters. For those who preferred a private pool, Gray's Baths of Fulton Street served that purpose. They touted "briny waters of the great deep that ebb and flow continuously," and guaranteed that a plunge or two into the depths would not only cleanse the body but also invigorate the frame. Although the visitor may enter in a "melting mood," he would soon leave "cool as a cucumber."[15]

For those more athletically inclined a new participatory sport had sprung up in the late 1850s, when the game of base ball took the public's fancy. Its widespread popularity sparked the rapid spread of base ball organizations, and by 1854 New York had four base ball clubs: the Knickerbockers, Gothams, Eagles, and Empires. A foursome from Brooklyn soon joined them: the Excelsiors, Putnams, Eckfords, and Atlantics. From 1858 until 1867 the Atlantics captured the acclaimed "whip" pennant, except in 1862 and 1863 when the Eckfords won it. The championship matches took place at the Fashion Race Course on Long Island, a site now in Queens' East Elmhurst, directly across from La Guardia Airport. Capacity crowds paid fifty cents each to watch the games. By 1856 it seemed that playing fields covered every available lot within the city limits. Brooklyn, already known as the "city of churches" looked more and more like the "city of base ball fields."[16]

In 1862 the first wooden ball park rose near the Union Hall grounds in Williamsburg, and it soon became the new home of the Eckfords, who had played at the old Manor House ball field in East Williamsburg until then. The Atlantics played on Putnam Avenue near Wild's Tavern and moved to the Capitoline Grounds in 1863, the field being bounded by Halsey, Myrtle, Putnam, and Nostrand avenues. The Excelsiors played on a vacant lot between Smith, Carroll, Hoyt, and President streets. The Putnams played on a field far out on Putnam Avenue where it met Broadway, and the Continentals played at Wheat Hill, located at Bedford and Lee avenues and Rush Street.[17]

In 1860 Brooklyn's Excelsior team visited cities in Central and Western New York State, a trip remarkable not only as the first base ball tour, but also because of the team's success. The games at Troy, Albany, and Buffalo gained so many new adherents that base ball's success spread rapidly, and many new teams joined in the competition. In 1861 at the annual convention of the base ball fraternity, David Milliken announced that fifty-six clubs sent representatives and the annual report showed four hundred dollars in the treasury, money that would be divided among the players who had volunteered to soldier during the Civil War. With three newly admitted clubs Brooklyn now had sixteen teams, including the Excelsiors, Atlantics, Eckfords, Hamilton, Star, Independents, Charter Oak, Exercise, Brooklyn, Powhattan, Olympic of South Brooklyn, Favorites, Resolute, Constellation, Putnam, and Continentals.[18]

The daily war news created a rollercoaster ride of emotions for patriotic Brooklynites. Despite their gloom on hearing of the federal debacle at Bull Run in 1861, or of the painful Union defeat at Chancellorsville in 1863, they gained distraction by watching a thrilling base ball game or by listening to banjo music. When word of a triumph reached them, as when the Brooklyn-built <u>Monitor</u> thwarted the Confederate ironclad <u>Merrimac</u>'s attempt to destroy the federal blockading squadron in 1862, they sang patriotic songs at musical shows. The Civil War, its horrors notwithstanding, apparently boosted rather than hurt Brooklyn's leisure time activities.

[1] <u>Growing Up In Brooklyn</u>, pp.6,9.
   <u>Phoenix Happy Birthday BAM</u> issue, 1986.

[2] Brooklyn <u>Eagle</u>, January 23, 1861.
   <u>Growing Up In Brooklyn</u>, p.7.

[3] Laura Keene was onstage in <u>Our American Cousin</u>, at
   Ford's Theatre, in Washington, D.C., when John Wilkes
   Booth shot and killed President Abraham Lincoln.

[4] Brooklyn <u>Era</u>, December 28, 1861.
   <u>Growing Up In Brooklyn</u>, pp.8, 9.
   Odell, George C., <u>Annals of the New York Stage</u>(N.Y.,
   1931), 15 vol., vol.3, pp.531, 532.
   <u>Phoenix</u>, p.3.
   Brooklyn Academy of Music information bulletin, pp.2,3.

[5] Brooklyn <u>Eagle</u>, October 24, 1863.

[6] <u>Ibid</u>.

[7] Brooklyn <u>Standard</u>, October 31, 1863.

[8] Brooklyn Academy of Music information bulletin.

[9] Brooklyn <u>Standard</u>, September 19, 1863.
   <u>Annals of the New York Stage</u>, pp.612, 613.

[10] Brooklyn <u>Standard</u>, June 3,20, 1861.
   <u>Annals of the New York Stage</u>, p.455.
   <u>The City of Brooklyn A Political History</u>, p.23.

[11] Charles Stratton (General Tom Thumb), the star of P. T.
   Barnum's museum in New York was thirty-two inches tall.

[12] Annals of the New York Stage, pp.534, 536, 538.

Brooklyn Era, December 21, 1861.

Brooklyn Eagle, April 25, 1861.

McKay, Ernest A., The Civil War and New York City,(Syracuse,1990), p.180.

[13] Brooklyn Eagle, April 25, 1861.

Brooklyn Era, December 12, 1861.

Annals of the New York Stage, p. 708.

People of Brooklyn, p.26.

[14] Brooklyn Era, January 11, 1862.

[15] Brooklyn Eagle, July 9, 1861.

[16] Seymour, Harold, Baseball, the Early Days(N.Y., 1960), pp.22,24,25.

Spalding, Albert G., America's National Game(N.Y., 1911), pp.79, 91-93.

[17] The History of the City of Brooklyn, edited by Henry W.B.Howard, Brooklyn, 1893, 2 vol., vol.2, pp.10, 11.

[18] Brooklyn Era, December 21, 1861.

America's National Game, p.79.

INDUSTRY

Civil War Brooklyn's diverse industrial activities took place along its winding shoreline, especially in Greenpoint and Williamsburg. These neighborhoods specialized in the five black arts, named so because of their smoky by-products: glassmaking, pottery, printing, cast-iron manufacturing, and petroleum refining.[1]

The city's production capacities were prodigious. It manufactured iron bedsteads, railings, awning posts, spectacles, corsets, millinery, blinds, stoves, men's and boy's clothing, cut glass, cabinets, pianos, wire, barometers, pharmaceuticals, boots and shoes, lamp oil, chimney globes, and thermometers. Companies made felt, hats, oilcloth, macaroni, hemp, chocolate, mustard, vinegar, sashes, and printing ink. They handled tobacco, chemicals, steamsaws, files, and cement. There were tanneries, fat-boiling establishments, and stone-cutting yards. Factories produced mineral water, metal leaf, sulphur, cloth, lamps, morocco, boxes, matches, and soda water. There were slaughterhouses, rosin-oil distilleries, breweries, coal yards, brick yards and foundries, truss makers and umbrella manufacturers, sausage makers, daguerreotypists, bird and beast stuffers, scavengers (later called antique dealers), gold beaters, ambrotypists, plasterers, house and sign painters. Oculists and dentists offered their services, as did Madame Morrow, who imported the latest Paris fashions. Entrepeneurs made soaps, candles, monuments, vaults, carriages, wagons, heaters, and engines to drive sewing machines. And in 1863 manufacturers added sportsmen's guns, fishing tackle, ice skates, cricketing implements, and artificial human eyes and limbs, the latter two by-products of the awful war that had been raging for two long years.[2]

Warehouses, docks, basins, and shipyards lined the Brooklyn waterfront. The Atlantic Dock Company, with piers, storage houses, and grain elevators had properties valued at over three million dollars and formed one of America's largest depots for receiving, storing, and transshipping western grain. It handled more than fifty million dollars worth of that commodity and other merchandise in a single year and became, in effect, the terminal of the Erie Canal. One pier extended three thousand feet into Buttermilk Channel and could handle the largest ship afloat.[3]   On June 3, 1861, eighty-nine vessels lay at anchor in the Atlantic Basin including nineteen ships, forty barks, twenty brigs and ten schooners. Sixty-three of them loaded or unloaded grain, but others carried guano, molasses, and sugar. Some had nothing to do with northern commerce. They were blockade-runners captured as a result of President Lincoln's April 19 edict ordering a blockade of southern ports. Four prize ships, all filled to the brim with cotton and tobacco, would have their cargo sold at auction and the proceeds divided between the government and the officers and crew of the capturing blockade enforcement vessels.[4]

Edward Robinson Squibb, founder of the pharmaceutical company that bears his name, served as a navy doctor after his graduation from medical school in 1845. He manufactured drugs for the government at the Brooklyn Naval Hospital and in 1858, after his discharge, he rented a five-story building at 149 Furman Street, set up a laboratory, and began to manufacture chemicals.

An old friend, Dr. Richard S. Satterlee, the army's chief medical purveyor for New York, felt that a Republican victory in 1860 meant war, and he discussed with Squibb the idea of producing bandages and splints. After Fort Sumter's fall, army contracts became the mainstay of Squibb's business, and increasing volume forced him to rent additional buildings on Columbia and Vine Streets. He also built another factory at 36 Doughty Street where his innovative mechanical devices for the mixing of special formulas played a pioneering role in the creation of pharmaceutical production lines.[5]

For the week ending April 18, 1863, with business booming, Squibb employed forty-four workers who produced what amounted to eight per cent of all federal army purchases. Panniers (medicine cases) formed the bulk of his trade, and he made them not only for Satterlee but also for the medical purveyor of Philadelphia. Since the war's beginning, Squibb had delivered forty thousand dollars worth of panniers and had accepted new orders totaling five thousand dollars to ten thousand dollars more. Another important product, ether, served both sides, regularly appearing behind southern lines through clandestine means. If President Lincoln knew of this, he turned a blind eye for humanitarian reasons.[6]

Another chemist also started his business in Brooklyn. Emigrating from the German states in 1848, Charles Pfizer established his plant in Williamsburg, then an independent German-speaking community. With twenty-five hundred dollars borrowed from his father, he bought a brick building on Bartlett Street in order to manufacture chemicals. Pfizer combined his skills as a chemist with those of his cousin,

Charles Erhard, a confectioner, in order to render medicines more palatable. The first creation, Santonin, a compound to combat parisitic worms, looked like a candy cone and had a sugar cream to hide its bitter taste.[7]

During the Civil War the demand for drugs and chemicals rose sharply as protective wartime tariffs raised the cost of European imports. In 1863 Pfizer imported crude argols (the wine cask residue) and set up their own operations to manufacture cream of tartar and tartaric acid used as a food preservative by bakers, beverage makers, and housewives. Rochelle salt, frequently used by physicians as a diuretic and cathartic and by industry for plating and mirror manufacturing also became another successful Pfizer item.[8]

In 1972 the Pfizer Company reached its billion dollar sales milestone. Chairman of the Board of Directors John J. Powers, Jr. pointed out that Pfizer's empire of eighty-eight plants in thirty-five countries, with sales offices in more than one hundred, had all started in a small brick building on Brooklyn's Bartlett Street.[9]

As early as the 1600s Kings County had a pottery near the local taverns that served patrons near the ferry landings and for the next two hundred years stoneware and earthenware potteries operated in Brooklyn. During the Civil War the industry thrived.[10]

In 1861 and 1862 Thomas Boone and Thomas Burns used one fire and eight employees to produce six hundred drain pipes, fourteen thousand pots and fourteen thousand furnaces. Williamsburg Pottery, begun in 1864 by Henry Oberhauser, produced chemical wares along with plumbing supplies, cooking ware, drainpipes, and flowerpots.[11]

In 1861 New York architect Thomas C. Smith bought a one- kiln pottery on Eckford Street which produced soft-paste porcelain. Smith had purchased it as a financial investment but soon became curious about production methods. He arranged to import the fine clay, kaolin, from Cornwall, England, and bought a feldspar quarry at home. Then he built a shop so that he could produce his own machinery and tools. The protective Morrill Tariff law of 1861 and later tariff increases gave American potteries an advantage over their foreign competition. Throughout the Civil War years, while producing soft-paste porcelain, hardware trimmings, door knobs, vases, and dishes, Smith's potters experimented with hard-paste porcelain, which is composed of kaolin and the mineral feldspar. When heated, the materials fuse, becoming glass-like, and produce fine-grained, translucent, non-absorbent porcelain, greatly different from earthenware. Called china, porcelain generally falls into two categories: hard paste (true porcelain) and soft paste. Hard-paste porcelain, beautiful and long lasting, serves as tableware, doorknobs, and hardware trimmings, and its glaze and translucence make it perfect for vases and objets d'art. In 1865 Smith's company produced its first true porcelain. For a goodly portion of the late nineteeth century the Union Porcelain Works remained the only pottery in the United States making this product.[12]

The Brooklyn Flint Glass Works, established in 1832 at Columbia and District (Atlantic Avenue) streets, made high quality, easily cut flint glass products. In 1864 the works produced blown, cut, and pressed glassware "of all sizes and colors suitable for the manufacturing of buttons, dress trimmings, etc." When the company relocated upstate in 1869 it changed its name to the Corning Glass Works.[13]

Christian Dorflinger's Plymouth Street Long Island Flint Company started in 1836. Known for its fine quality and its unique engravings it had many wealthy patrons including Mary Todd Lincoln, who ordered a table setting for the White House.[14]

The glass industry used child labor and Dorflinger counted forty youngsters among its workforce of one hundred and five. Boys usually performed general factotum jobs in the furnace room where temperatures ran over one hundred degrees in the summer, while girls worked in the finishing departments.[15]

Until the 1850s the coloring in illustrated books had to be brushed on by hand. Families worked on them at home, each child applying a different color. McLoughlin Brothers, a leading publisher of children's books and paper cut-out dolls, moved to Brooklyn for more room. In the early 1860s they experimented with a new process of photoengraving from zinc plates. This photomechanical innovation enabled the firm to publish inexpensive children's books with colored illustrations, as well as card games, board games, coloring books, cut-out paper dollhouses, and valentines.[16]

Another publisher came to Brooklyn to escape the overcrowding of Manhattan. Pioneer manufacturer Alfred S. Barnes produced and distributed school books, and his national series of standard primers had tremendous success. When he lost the lucrative southern market during the Civil War, he turned to the west and exploited that hitherto untapped region. During Reconstruction the Freedman's Bureau adopted his national series for use in black schools in the southern states.[17]

The Havemeyer family refined sugar, and had a monthly payroll of one hundred thousand dollars. By utilizing and improving the most advanced European methods, Havemeyer and Elder, located near South 4th Street and 1st Avenue in Williamsburg, became one of the largest sugar refineries in the world, capable of shipping over four hundred thousand barrels a year.[18]

A. A. Low became the country's largest importer of tea, and Elias Howe, Jr.,the first American to obtain a patent on the sewing machine[19] sold his product from his home on Washington Street.[20]

Peter Cooper, founder of Cooper Union, ran a glue factory near 23rd Street in Manhattan. He claimed that he went from "nothing to affluence through hard work." In 1838 the constant criticism of his malodorous by-products prodded him to buy a ten-acre plot north of the Maspeth Turnpike in the Bushwick section of Brooklyn for two hundred dollars. The quality of his glues made his product highly desirable in the manufacture of books, furniture, and pianofortes, not only here but in England, too. In 1869 his firm became the largest manufacturer of glue and gelatin in the world. A secretive man, Cooper divulged no information concerning his yearly output. He issued no balance sheets or earning statements, and his grandson insisted that "the old man knew to the penny each day's cash balance and what bills were due." His profits, although unknown, were so great that he became a millionaire in his mid- sixties. During the Civil War, and the arrival of the first income tax, he paid five thousand three hundred and forty-one dollars to the government on an income of one hundred six thousand eighty hundred seventy-nine dollars.[21]

Brooklyn's industrial might proved a major weapon during the Civil War. As the terminal of the Erie Canal the city's dockside facilities shipped to Europe one of the Union's greatest weapons - grain - a commodity that became more and more important to England's welfare. Prior to 1861 England imported less than one quarter of her grain from America. The situation, however, changed completely when western Europe experienced crop failures in the early 1860s. Through 1861 and 1862 America's share of England's grain imports had risen to nearly half. In addition, to prevent southern naval raiders, like the much-feared Alabama, from preying on grain-laden ships, the cargo was placed on English vessels. Not only was England now dependent on America's produce but the use of their own ships proved a big plus in their own economy. These two factors became paramount when England had to choose whether or not to recognize the Confederacy, an action that might have altered the outcome of the war to the detriment of the federal government.[22]

[1] Brooklyn Almanac, p.57.
[2] Map of the city of Brooklyn, 1855, N.Y.P.L. Map Room.
The City of Brooklyn A Political History, p.14.
Brooklyn City Directory, 1860.
Brooklyn Almanac, p.57.
The Brooklyn Neighborhood Book, p.57.
[3] The City of Brooklyn A Political History, pp.13,14.
Miller's New York As It Is, p.110.

Growing Up in Brooklyn, p.8.

[4] Brooklyn Standard, June 3, 1861.
Civil War Dictionary, p.70.

[5] Blochman, Lawrence C., Dr.Squibb(N.Y., 1958), pp. vii,1,112,115,131,132.
Smith, George Winston, The Squibb Laboratory in 1863, The Journal of the History of Medicine, July,1958, p.382.
Letter from Wilbur B. McDowell, Squibb Company archivist, August 12,1986.

[6] Wickware, Francis Sill, The House of Squibb(N.Y., 1965), pp.135,136.
Smith, George Winston, Medicines For The Union Army(Madison, Wisc.,1962), pp.23-25.

[7] Mines, Samuel, Pfizer, An Informal History(N.Y., 1978), pp.1-4.

[8] Ibid., pp. 1-4,7.

[9] Ibid.

[10] Corbett, Cynthia, Useful Art Long Island Pottery(N.Y., 1985), pp.50,51.

[11] Useful Art Long Island Pottery, p.55.

[12] Factories, Foundries and Refineries, p.21,22,27,28,37.
Useful Art Long Island Pottery, pp.56,57.
Weiss, Gustav, The Book of Porcelain(Berlin,1964), translated by Janet Seligman, p.183.

[13] Corning Glass Works Historical Timeline.
Brooklyn city directory, 1864

[14] Factories, Foundries and Refineries, pp.13-17.

[15] Ibid.

[16] Ibid.p.38.

[17] Ibid. p.40.

[18] Havemeyer family records, N.Y.H.S.

The City of Brooklyn A Political History, p.14.

[19] Benjamin F. Butler served as his attorney.

[20] New York Times, October 3,1867.
Starfield, Martin J., Highlights of Brooklyn
Heights(Brooklyn, 1987), p.18.

[21] Mack, Edward C., Peter Cooper, Citizen of New York(N.Y.,
1949), pp.79-81,195,308.

[22] Battle Cry of Freedom, pp.386,817.

SHIPBUILDING

In 1781 three brothers -- John, Samuel, and Treadwell Jackson -- bought a large tract of land in northeast Brooklyn. The purchase included a few dilapidated buildings formerly used for assembling ships, a pond where wood was aged and seasoned, and a small island with a pier. This modest spot would one day become the Brooklyn Navy Yard,[1] the largest industrial plant in New York State. It covered two hundred ninety acres and contained two hundred seventy buildings, all connected by nineteen miles of paved roads and thirty-nine miles of railroad track. It also had six dry docks, eight piers, and many giant warehouses and lumber yards, making it one of America's largest shipbuilding and maritime repair units.[2]

The Jacksons built the frigate <u>Adams</u> in 1798, the first government-financed vessel, and the yard soon became a repair depot as well as a shipbuilding facility. By the end of the War of 1812 it had fitted out and supplied more than a hundred ships.[3]

During the Civil War the yard converted and outfitted four hundred and sixteen vessels purchased by the government for use as warships, supply vessels or blockaders. One passenger ship, the <u>Monticello</u>, underwent a rapid metamorphosis. Workers ripped out her silk tapestries, velvet hangings, and inlaid panels and set up her armament and fully equipped her for war service within twenty-four hours.[4]

By the summer of 1861 an average of sixteen hundred fifty laborers and mechanics worked daily, earning some six hundred seventy-nine thousand dollars. After four years of war and heavy government sponsorship in shipbuilding, these figures had jumped to six thousand men and a payroll of more than four million dollars.[5]

On November 20, 1861, the yard made its first contribution to the Union navy by launching the screw steam sloop Oneida, which later participated in the battles of New Orleans (1862) and Mobile Bay (1864). Severely hit during the latter engagement, she fought alongside other Brooklyn-built ships, the six-gun side-wheeler Octorora and the nine-gun steamer Lackawanna. The shipyard also built the warships Adirondack, Ticonderoga, Shamrock, Mackinaw, Peoria, Tullahoma, Maumee, Nyack, and Wampanoag, and the ironclad Mianonomah.[6]

The Confederates knew of the yard's importance and planned a raid against it. At least that is what local officials feared. They learned that groups of Confederate sympathizers would rendezvous near the Navy Yard and hurl incendiaries into the facility's imflammable stores. Captain (later Commodore) Andrew H. Foote, second in command to Rear Admiral Samuel Livingston Breese, learned of the plot, conferred with Mayor Samuel Powell, and deployed both the yard's sailors and the metropolitan police. Soon one thousand policemen took positions near the Navy Yard and the ferry terminals while police boats and armed men in rowboats patrolled the river. Colonel Graham's Seventieth Artillery Regiment took possession of the Portland Avenue Armory in case rebel sympathizers try to raid it for weapons. Colonel Smith's Thirteenth Regiment secured the armory on Cranberry Street while General Duryea's militia stood ready. The defenses sprang up so quickly that no attempt to attack the yard ever materialized. The mayor and Captain Foote firmly believed a real danger had existed, but many scoffers always referred to the incident as the "Navy Yard scare."[7]

In 1850 Eckford Webb opened a shipyard in Greenpoint known as Webb and Bells, and for the next twenty years, thirty-five per cent of Greenpoint's working population built ships. Throughout the Civil War carpenters labored in ten yards along Greenpoint's shoreline building vessels whose value exceeded ten million dollars. Day and night workers assembled both small skiffs and large schooners. Huge quantities of white oak, hackamatack, locust, and yellow and white pine formed enormous lumber piles awaiting use for ribs, keelsons, ceiling timber, decks, floors, and aprons. The odor of this man-made forest filled the air, and the continual hammering and sawing created a constant din. Laborers moved in nearby with their families, attracted by the steady work which initially consisted of fifteen hours daily for one dollar and twenty-five cents. Later, labor organizations secured a ten-hour day, and wages rose to two dollars, an excellent salary in the 1860s. Many men, however, went from yard to home totally exhausted, ate, slept, and began the cycle again the next morning. A particularly nasty job was using the ubiquitous two-man saw, which required one worker in the pit, his face covered by a handkerchief protecting him from the sawdust, and his partner above. As there were no cranes, cables, or mechanical power, men lifted the heaviest timbers, doing this work in teams. [8]

Many of Greenpoint's shipyards worked around the clock. Thomas Rowland's Continental Iron Works built the warships Montauk, Passaic, Catskill, Onondaga, Cohoes,

Purita, Puritan, Monadnock, and Muscootah. The Dry Dock Ironworks, established by J. S. Underhill, built the light draught Mordoc, for coast service. In 1864 Henry Steers built the sloop Idaho, a vessel of three thousand tons, three hundred feet long, forty-four feet wide, with a twenty-foot deep hold. Launched in the summer, it had two propellers, contained engines of three thousand horsepower and won regard as an unusually speedy addition to the United States Navy.[9]

Although Brooklyn's Navy Yard and its other shipyard facilities made many important contributions to the federal war effort, the Continental Iron Works' production of one particular vessel dwarfed all other achievements. During the winter of 1861-1862 it built the Monitor.

[1] Officially the New York Naval Shipyard.
[2] West, James H., A Short History of the Naval Yard (Brooklyn, 1941), p.216.
   The New York Naval Shipyard Sesquicentennial Anniversary Souvenir Journal, undated, B.H.S.
[3] Ibid.
[4] Ibid.
[5] Ibid.
[6] Ibid.
[7] The History of the City of Brooklyn, (Stiles), vol.2, pp.441,442.
[8] Historic Greenpoint, William L. Felter, pamphlet, 1919, B.H.S. p.29.
   Hoehling, A.A., Thunder at Hampton Roads (Englewood Cliffs), p.60.
[9] Brooklyn Life, LIX, April 26, 1919.

THE MONITOR

From the outbreak of the Civil War, the Confederate government realized it could not compete with a rapidly expanding Union navy. Forced to innovate, they created a maritime monster which Confederate Secretary of the Navy Stephen Mallory felt would be invulnerable to attack. Union spies alerted Washington that the Union ship Merrimac, scuttled by federal forces hurriedly fleeing the Norfolk, Virginia, navy yard, had been raised and rebuilt by the rebels into an ironclad ram[1] renamed the Virginia. Her official name never caught on; even Confederates referred to it as the Merrimac.[2]

A concerned federal secretary of the navy, Gideon Welles, immediately advertised for plans for a similar vessel. These notices caught the attention of Cornelius Scranton Bushnell, owner of a Mystic, Connecticut, shipyard, who obtained a contract for the Galena, a conventional warship which would be given metallic protection. Since few people had expertise with this new technique, he followed a recommendation from fellow contractor Cornelius Delamater and sought out the most knowledgable man in the field, a cantankerous Swedish inventor named John Ericsson, of Beach Street in New York. From their meeting came a Brooklyn-built ship that would alter naval warfare forever.[3]

A former naval cadet and army engineer, Ericsson had trained on Sweden's Gota Canal, studying the behavior of raft-like boats during local storms. A powerfully-built man, once a weight lifter and wrestler, he appeared much younger than his fifty-eight years. He also possessed an indomitable will and little patience for dissent, generally paying scant attention to what others thought. Ericsson had invented and built air compressors, boilers, engines, locomotives, the prototype for a screw propeller, and naval guns. With a partner, Captain Robert S. Stockton of the United States Navy, he designed a man-of-war, the Princeton, and was involved in a tragic accident that would color his relationship with the department of the navy for almost twenty years. The Princeton carried another Ericsson invention, a twelve-caliber gun, the biggest ever to be used by a fighting ship. Stockton had forged his own version of the weapon, but without Ericsson's special reinforcements, it was weak at its sides. Stockton placed his gun on board the Princeton and called it the "Peacemaker." On February 28, 1844, President John Tyler and members of his cabinet came aboard to see it in action. Stockton repeatedly fired the "Peacemaker," much to the amusement of his guests. His last shot, however, overstrained the weakened sides and the weapon exploded, killing Secretary of State Abel P. Upshur and Secretary of the Navy Thomas Gilmer. President Tyler, having remained below with other guests was unharmed. Stockton tried to blame his partner, but Ericsson demonstrated successfully that the weapon, properly reinforced, would not have exploded as the "Peacemaker" did. The navy brass, however, never forgave nor forgot and developed a fear of any more of Ericsson's innovations.[4]

Ericsson advised Bushnell about the Galena and then showed him plans and a scale model for a craft he had developed for Napoleon III of France. Ericsson described his invention as an "impregnable steam battery of light draught," which would float with its deck nearly awash, its hull tapered at each side, and her eleven-inch Dahlgren guns mounted side by side in a revolving turret. He had written to President Lincoln in August 1861, describing his invention, but had never received a response.[5]

Bushnell sensed a patriotic yet profitable venture, and he hurried home to see his neighbor, Gideon Welles. Bushnell enthusiastically described a possible antidote to the Merrimac's threat, and Welles sent him to Washington for a meeting with the ironclad board, comprised of three naval traditionalists: Commodores Joseph Smith and Hiram Paulding and Commander Charles H. Davis.[6]

The navy brass, however, proved immune to Bushnell's blandishments, and Davis even ridiculed the model. Undaunted by this setback, and through the intercession of John F. Winslow and John Griswold, friends of Secretary of State William Henry Seward, Bushnell met with another inventor, President Abraham Lincoln (Lincoln held patent number 6,469, for the creation of buoyant chambers to lift boats over shoals.[7]) The president liked Ericsson's invention and reconvened the naval board, but Davis proved immune to even the president's urgings, deeming the craft unseaworthy. Lincoln rose from the plain box he had used as a seat and announced, "Well, as the girl said when she put her leg in the stocking, I think there is something in it."[8]

The resourceful Bushnell raced back to New York to see Ericsson. Mentioning no particular setback, Bushnell said that Davis had proffered arguments that he could not address and that it would be important for Ericsson to appear in person. The Swede, who could be as charming and persuasive as he was egotistical and arrogant, left immediately for the capital. The next day he turned in a bravura performance, lecturing the naval board on seaworthiness and stability. Greatly impressed, yet hesitant over the memory of the Princeton fiasco, the board nevertheless made him an offer, albeit a very cautious one. The contract guaranteed complete success or a refund of all government money paid. The new partners -- Winslow, Griswold, Bushnell, and Ericsson -- would receive two hundred seventy-five thousand dollars,[9] if the government received delivery within one hundred days. It seemed impossible, and perhaps the spiteful ironclad board secretly hoped the project would fail, but Ericsson's powerful ego allowed no doubt about eventual success. Work began immediately.[10]

The hull would be built at Thomas F. Rowland's Continental Iron Works on Calyer Street, in the Greenpoint section of Brooklyn; the plates, bars, and rivets would be supplied by two upstate New York firms, Winslow's Albany Iron Works of Troy, and Griswold's Iron Works of Rensselaer. The Delamater Iron Works of New York's West Street would manufacture the steam machinery, boilers, and propellers; and the Novelty Iron Works would build the unique revolving turret. The group would pay inventor Theodore Timby five thousand dollars for each turret used, even though Timby's patent would not be granted until September 1862. Ericsson bristled at giving Timby anything. The idea of a revolving turret, he said, had been around since his youth. However, pressured by the others he reluctantly agreed.[11]

For the next three months Ericsson hovered over the Ironworks' men, supervising, bullying, praising, and encouraging them to work night and day for his creation. Miraculously, in 101 days, the Monitor slid into the water on

January 30, 1862, and proceeded to the Brooklyn Navy Yard for further fitting. One hundred seventy-two feet long, it drew ten and one-half feet of water and would soon have two eleven inch smoothbore Dahlgren guns placed in its revolving turret.[12]

Ericsson wrote to Assistant Secretary of the Navy Gustavus Fox that "the ironclad intruder will prove a severe monitor not only to the southern rebels but also to Downing Street," a reference to the British government,[13] and thus the vessel's unusual name, which in no time became generic for all ironplated warships. Sixty-seven Monitor-type vessels were launched throughout the war, seven being built at the Continental Iron Works.[14]

Ironclad board member Commodore Joseph Smith exerted influence to gain the new ship's command for a family friend, John Lorimer Worden, an upstate New Yorker.[15] With fifty-six volunteers, (the navy deemed the project too risky for regular sailors), Worden and his twenty-year-old executive officer, Lieutenant Samuel Dana Greene, familiarized themselves with what would prove to be a very different kind of vessel.[16]

The Monitor's trial run revealed many defects, which Ericsson easily corrected. He personally attended to problems in the steering, the engines, and the cut-off valves, while Chief Engineer Alban Stimers adjusted the ship's compasses. Finally, on March 6, 1862, escorted by the gunboats Carrittuck and Sachem and the tug Seth Low, the Monitor left the navy yard headed for the Atlantic Ocean and a harrowing journey to Hampton Roads, Virginia, at the entrance to Chesapeake Bay.[17] After a smooth first day, the rest of the Monitor's trip turned into a nightmare. A violent storm struck, causing unusually rough seas, and the vessel nearly foundered. Her engines stopped because of lack of steam, and the furnace blower belts broke repeatedly, causing a lack of ventilation, a combination of events that created a potentially fatal mixture of carbon dioxide. Engineers attempting to correct the defects continually passed out until Stimers, almost overcome by fumes himself, finally gained control by using relays of men working for brief periods.[18]

About 2:00 p.m. on March 8, the reconditioned Merrimac had sailed into Hampton Roads and attacked the federal blockading squadron. She quickly proved her formidability by ramming the thirty-gun Cumberland and raking the fifty-gun Congress with fire. Within an hour and a half the Cumberland sank and the Congress surrendered. In an effort to help, the Minnesota had run aground and since the tide had ebbed, the Merrimac could not get to her. These three wooden Union warships represented the best the federal navy could offer, with three hundred guns to face the Confederate vessel's ten. The Merrimac, however, shrugging off it enemies' shot, had smashed the Union fleet with her own fire or her powerful ram. The Confederate iron-clad retired for the night at 5:00 p.m. planning to return the next morning to finish off the grounded Minnesota.[19]

The Monitor arrived at Hampton Roads at 9:00 p.m. and saw the smoke-filled sky, the silhouette of the burning Congress, and the mast of the sunken Cumberland. Worden sent a man ashore to wire Secretary of the Navy Gideon Welles of his plan to proceed to the assistance of the Minnesota.[20]

When the Merrimac returned the next morning to destroy the Minnesota she spied a small vessel lying alongside.

110

Confederate seamen, puzzled by the craft's strange appearance, dubbed it a "Cheesebox on a Raft," and thought she might be some sort of water tender. The rebels saw a ship with no sails, no smokestack, and no visible guns. When the Merrimac closed to a half a mile, however, they saw the odd craft pull away from the Minnesota, open her turret and spit fire. The first shot missed its mark, but the second struck home, rocking the Merrimac. Confederate Captain Franklin Buchanan recognized Ericsson's battery, as the Confederates called her, and pulled closer to attack. The rebel ship dwarfed its Federal opponent, being a hundred feet longer, with ten guns to the Monitor's two, but she was a clumsy craft and took a half hour to turn around, a maneuver the Monitor made in one sixth the time. This advantage in mobility made the odds close to even.[21]

For three and a half hours the two armored vessels blasted each other, often at distances of only fifty to one hundred yards. Each time the rebels tried to hit the guns of the Monitor's twenty foot turret, it revolved, showing no more than a blank iron wall. All too often the smaller craft would turn and twist, making a difficult target. At one point, while the Monitor reloaded, the Merrimac slipped by and raked the stranded Minnesota before running aground. On seeing this the Monitor approached more closely and received a shot that exploded just outside the pilot house, blinding Captain Worden, the Monitor's only casualty, and putting Lieutenant Greene in charge.[22]

The Merrimac, after some anxious moments, freed herself and limped towards her consorts, the Jamestown and Yorktown, while Greene broke off the struggle and headed back to guard the Minnesota. This abrupt change of plans may have saved the Merrimac from disaster. Her unarmored lower sides, now visible, were highly vulnerable to hits that would have opened her wooden ribs and sunk her had the Yankee gunners lowered their sights. But Greene, fearing that new damage to his pilot house would cripple the experimental vessel, felt responsible for keeping the navy's most valuable ship intact. He decided against continuing the battle, a decision for which he was roundly criticized.[23]

With twenty-two hits, several inflicted by the Minnesota in its attempt to even the score with the Merrimac, the Monitor's greatest damage lay in the pilot house, which controlled her steering. Her gun crews, totally inexperienced, had done well, firing forty-one shots at its giant opponent, twenty of which struck home. The Confederate ironclad, her engines barely operating and suffering from severe water damage, seemed in no condition to continue the fight. Both sides called it quits, each claiming victory. John Ericsson felt cheated. The navy's ordinance department had allowed only fifteen pounds of powder in each charge of the Monitor's eleven inch Dahlgren guns instead of the thirty pounds the inventor had insisted on. Ericsson believed that with the proper charge the Merrimac would have been sunk in fifteen minutes.[24]

President Lincoln met with his cabinet, congratulated them on the "victory," and wired Bushnell to prepare six more ironclads. The blockade of the industry-poor south that the president instituted held, and the north built sixty-seven more "Monitors" that would prove their worth many times over during the war. The success of the two iron-clads spelled the doom of wooden navies and forced the creation of a new generation of fighting ships.[25]

The Merrimac never fought again. The Confederates destroyed her in May 1862 to avoid her capture by federal forces. The Monitor, heading south on New Year's Eve 1862, lost her tow line, foundered, and sank in a storm off Cape Hatteras, North Carolina. Lieutenant Greene and forty-eight others survived.[26] Blind in one eye and with a permanently blackened face, John L. Worden continued his navy career, retiring as an admiral in 1886. Lieutenant Greene believed the government never properly appreciated his efforts. In 1884, during a tour as equipment officer at the Portsmouth, New Hampshire, Naval Base he committed suicide. John Ericsson won well-deserved honors as a premier inventor; his novel vessel had at least forty new patents. He died in 1889 and, as he had requested, the government returned his body to Sweden for interment. Chief Engineer Alban Stimers, whom Ericsson gave credit for keeping the Monitor afloat, helped in the construction of some thirty types of ironclads before his death in Staten Island in 1876.[27]

Seventeen years after the war's end, Congress voted a memorial, not to exceed two hundred thousand dollars, for the Monitor's officers and crew. The House of Representatives cited the great fear generated by the "scaled monster," the Merrimac, whose potential terror the Monitor stalemated. The Confederate ship, they asserted, could have destroyed the entire blockading squadron and ascended the Potomac River to lob bomb shells into the Capitol. No limits, they added, could be assigned to her destructive power, and the entire sea coast would have been at her mercy. The Senate bill, for the same purpose, mentioned the extreme hazards faced by the volunteer crew in this novel and untried ship. Predictions had poured in that the <u>Monitor</u> would never even make it to Hampton Roads, much less defeat the <u>Merrimac</u>, and therefore these men should be rewarded handsomely for their daring.[28]

Congress used as a precedent the case of the <u>Kearsarge</u>, whose officers and crew were granted the estimated value of the Confederate raider <u>Alabama</u>, which they had sunk off the French coast near Cherbourg. In this instance the amount came to one hundred ninety thousand dollars, based on a formula counting the worth of the enemy ship itself and one hundred dollars per man on the enemy's ship if of inferior force and two hundred dollars per man if of a superior force. Unhappily, the <u>Monitor</u>'s men never received their bonus. The debate continued from 1874 until 1885 when, as support dwindled, Congress permanently shelved the entire matter.[29]

After the <u>Monitor</u> sank, Paymaster William F. Keeler lamented, "What the fire of the enemy failed to do, the elements have accomplished." But the ironclad had enjoyed her hour of glory, one that would be rightly forever commemorated, for this unique Brooklyn-built ship had played an important role in saving the Union.[30]

In March 1974, the research ship <u>Alcoa Seaprobe</u>, using highly sophisticated underwater probing equipment, discovered the upside-down wreck of the <u>Monitor</u> in two hundred twenty feet of water off Cape Hatteras. Despite the difficulties of turbulent waters and dangerously changing currents, dredges brought up a host of <u>Monitor</u> artifacts. The National Register of Historic Places placed the ironclad on its list and in 1975 the government designated it as America's only historic marine sanctuary[31].

[1] A vessel with a powerful prow used to stave in the hull of wooden ships.

[2] Thunder at Hampton Roads, p.xvi.
How We Found The Monitor, John G. Newton, National Geographic, January 1975, p.56.
Battles and Leaders of the Civil War, edited by Robert U. Johnson and Clarence C. Buel, New York, 1884-1888 4 vol., vol. 1, p.712.

[3] How We Found The Monitor, p.56.
Wheeler, Francis B., The First Monitor and its Builders, (Poughkeepsie, N.Y. 1884), p.3.
Thunder at Hampton Roads, pp.41,42.

[4] Thunder at Hampton Roads, p.16,20,21.
Church, William C., The Life of John Ericsson(N.Y., 1911), pp.233,234,251.
White, Ruth, Yankee From Sweden(N.Y., 1960), pp.7,8, 111-115.
John Ericsson Society pamphlet, 1928, N.Y.H.S.

[5] Thunder at Hampton Roads, pp.42,43.
Yankee From Sweden, pp.189,190,191,197-202.
Life of John Ericsson, pp.246,247,249.

[6] Thunder at Hampton Roads, pp.41,42.

[7] Author's collection.

[8] Thunder at Hampton Roads, p.45.

[9] The partners turned an $80,000 profit.

[10] Cornelius Bushnell Association pamphlet, N.Y.H.S.
The Life of John Ericsson, p.253.
Yankee From Sweden, pp.109,197,199-202.

Neu, Irene D., <u>Erastus Corning, Merchant and Financier</u>(Ithaca, 1960), p.55.

[11] <u>Thunder at Hampton Roads</u>, p.53.

<u>The First Monitor and its Builders</u>, pp. 3,5,6.

<u>Monitor Companies; A Study of the Major Firms That Built the U.S.S. Monitor</u>, William H. Still, <u>American Neptune</u>, xlviii, number 2, Spring 1988, pp.107,111,121-123.

Davis, William C., <u>Duel Between the Ironclads</u>(Garden City, 1975), p.24.

[12] <u>Yankee From Sweden</u>, pp.205,206.

<u>The Life of John Ericsson</u>, p.255.

<u>Thunder at Hampton Roads</u>, p.60,69,70.

[13] Prior to emigrating to America, Ericsson had spent time in debtor's prison in London.

[14] <u>Battles and Leaders of the Civil War</u>, vol.1, p.731.

John Ericsson Society pamphlet, N.Y.H.S.

<u>The Life of John Ericsson</u>, p.254.

[15] Worden had spent time in an Alabama jail as the first federal prisoner of war.

[16] <u>The Monitor</u>, pamphlet, undated, Grand Army Plaza branch, Brooklyn Public Library.

Still, William S., <u>The Commanding Officers of the U.S.S. Monitor</u>(Greenville, N.C., 1988), pp.4,5.

[17] <u>Commanding Officers of the U.S.S. Monitor</u>, p.6.

Baxter, James P. 3rd, <u>The Introduction of the Ironclad Warship</u>(Hamden,Ct.,1968), pp 264-266.

<u>Life of John Ericsson</u>, pp.256,257.

[18] Letter from Alban C. Stimers to his father, May 5,1862, Buffalo Historical Society library, published by the Buffalo Civil War Round Table, as <u>A Rare Account From</u>

Aboard the Monitor.

Battles and Leaders, vol. 1, pp.720-722.

[19] Thunder At Hampton Roads, pp.107-116.

Battles and Leaders, vol. 1, pp.696-700.

Union naval losses that day were the worst in the country's history. Not until December 7, 1941, when the Japanese attacked Pearl Harbor, would it suffer such damage to its fleet.

[20] Thunder at Hampton Roads, pp. 107-116.

Battles and Leaders, vol. 1, pp.696-700.

[21] The Commanding Officers of the U.S.S. Monitor, pp.7,17,18.

Thunder at Hampton Roads, pp.107-116, 152-168.

Battles and Leaders, Vol. 1, pp.696-703.

[22] Thunder at Hampton Roads, pp.107-116.

Battles and Leaders, pp.726, 727.

[23] Thunder at Hampton Roads, pp.107-116.

Battles and Leaders, vol. 1, pp.703,727.

[24] Mokin, Arthur, Ironclad(Novato, California, 1991), pp.265,266.

Thunder at Hampton Roads, p.173.

New York Times, March 13, 1862.

Life of John Ericsson, pp.137,296.

Stimer's letter.

Battles and Leaders, vol.1, p.701.

[25] The History of the City of Brooklyn,(Stiles), vol.2, p.470.

Monitor file, B.P.L.

[26] Monitor National Marine Santuary Newsletter, February 14, ,1992.

Battles and Leaders, vol.1, pp.745-748.

[27] The Commanding Officers of the U.S.S. Monitor, pp. 8,22.

Stimer's letter.

Thunder At Hampton Roads, p.197.

[28] Abraham Lincoln, A Biography, p.309.

Report number one hundred forty-four, Forty-seventh Con gress, first session of the House of Representatives, 1882, B.H.S.

[29] Report number one hundred forty-four, Forty-seventh Congress.

Thunder at Hampton Roads, p.198.

[30] Monitor National Marine Sanctuary newsletter.

[31] How We Found The Monitor, p.61.

THE WAR BEGINS

The onset of the Civil War found Brooklyn in a state of near paralysis. Business came to a standstill when the shocking news of the attack on Fort Sumter arrived. This temporary inaction, however, soon gave way to displays of loyalty. Flags appeared in front of most stores and many private homes. One Williamsburg dwelling displayed a large flag along with a placard that announced: "The Union, the Constitution and the Enforcement of the Law." By official order all police stations raised the colors each morning, and when Father Rafina placed a flag atop his Montrose Avenue Catholic Church, a crowd of more than one thousand cheered him.[1]

The absence of "Old Glory" raised suspicions of disloyalty and southern sympathizers maintained a discreet silence as real danger existed in supporting secession. Firemen of Engine House Number One on Prospect Street hung an effigy of Confederate President Jefferson Davis, and at a Sunday meeting at Union Hall some German-Americans took umbrage at anti-government remarks made by a man named Smith. They decided to "teach him a lesson" and had a rope around his neck when friends interceded to set him free.[2]

For some though, greed exceeded patriotism. Officers Jacobs and Sherman of the Eastern District's sixth precinct discovered several tailor shops sewing Confederate army uniforms for Neutreck and Brothers of 4 Dey Street in New York, a company that had just been caught sending arms to the south in packages of clothing.[3]

Pro-Union sentiment, however, crystallized quickly

and resulted in public meetings and bellicose speeches. The president's call for volunteers resulted in the opening of nine recruiting tents in City Hall Park and others in Washington Park (Fort Greene) and the Navy Yard as existing militia regiments prepared for active duty.[4]

All enlisted men had to learn a new language, one that transformed old familiar words. "Arms" became "Umm;" "march" sounded like "utch;" a tent was a canvas; a sword a toadsticker. Mess beef translated into salt horse; coffee was boiled rye; vegetables were cow feed, and butter strong grease. "Bully" meant the highest praise, and "I don't see it" meant disapproval.[5]

The first Brooklyn unit ready for combat, the Thirteenth Regiment, under General Abraham Duryea and Colonel Abel Smith left the city on April 22, 1861. One of its drummer boys, Clarence Mackenzie, became Brooklyn's first casualty when he was killed in an accident in Annapolis, Maryland. His funeral on June 15 began at his parent's home on Liberty Street and wended its way along Concord and Fulton streets to St. John's Church on the corner of Washington and Johnson streets. Following a mournful sermon by the Reverend Dr. Guyon, young Mackenzie's casket, draped with an American flag and followed by a detachment of his outfit beating muffled drums, was taken to Green-Wood Cemetery for burial. Today a statue of the boy, complete with his drum, stands above his grave.[6]

One of the Thirteenth's men from the eastern district turned out not to be a man at all. Charles Marshall, a slim, effeminate youth, proved to be Maggie Wilson, listed missing from her home for the past two weeks. Even after this embarrassing revelation, the regiment kept its new recruit on as a cook.[7]

The Twenty-eighth Regiment, commanded by Colonel Michael Bennett, left for the front on April 28, after Sunday services. It carried with it fifteen hundred yards of bandages rolled by women of the Clinton Avenue Congregational Church. Upon arrival in the outskirts of Washington, the Twenty-eighth helped construct the earthworks that defended the Chain Bridge against rebel attack.[8]

In the Spring of 1861 the war department authorized Colonel Alfred M. Wood (1 Middagh Street) to recruit a regiment, and his Fourteenth State Militia became the Eighty-fourth New York Volunteers. The outfit gained fame, however, under its state name, the "Fourteenth Brooklyn," a title it bore with pride. The regiment departed on May 20 for the south, and this most famous of all Brooklyn outfits fought at both battles of Bull Run (1861 and 1862), Gettysburg (1863), the Wilderness (1864), and Spotsylvania (1864). Its commander, initially reported killed in action, had been captured in July 1861, but was released in time to return home and win election as mayor in 1863. The Fourteenth performed yeoman service in the Peninsula Campaign, and especially at Gettysburg, where not only did they help keep the rebels at bay during the battle's first day, but also captured Joseph R. Davis's Mississippi Brigade. The Fourteenth served for three years in Virginia and Maryland, suffering severe losses in several of its twenty-nine engagements before mustering out in June 1864 under the command of Colonel Edward B. Fowler.[9]

During the war the men of the Fourteenth gained a distinct nickname from their uniform, one patterned after the French Algerian light infantry, the Zouaves (pronounced Zwahves). They wore red flannel pants, a red vest, a navy blue flannel jacket and a red cap. This degree of high visibility and their esprit de corps earned them the sobriquet the "Red Legged Devils."[10]

Youths of the seventh, ninth, and nineteenth wards formed a volunteer company, and Captain William Hogan, former commander of the Napper Tandy Light Artillery, organized many of his fellow Irishmen into an artillery company that served with the First Regiment. Part of the famous Irish Brigade commanded by Colonel Robert Nugent, they carried a green flag in addition to the federal colors. Officially mustered into the service as the Sixty-ninth Infantry in the autumn of 1861, it had a goodly portion of Brooklyn men in its Company K.[11]

On August 22, the First Long Island Regiment, recruited by Colonel Nelson A. Cross and nicknamed the Brooklyn Phalanx, left for Washington, D.C., with one thousand men. Three years and fourteen battles later they came home on furlough to recruit, parading down Fulton Street to drum up interest. Only two hundred thirty-four men remained of the original group.[12]

Charles K. Graham, an engineer who built the drydocks and landings at the Brooklyn Navy Yard, enlisted with four hundred fellow workers. He served as the Colonel of the Seventy-fourth New York Regiment, received wounds at the Peach Orchard at Gettysburg, and became a brevet (temporary) major general of volunteers in 1865.[13] Colonel William Everdell of the Twenty-third Brooklyn Volunteers took his regiment to Gettysburg in July 1863, arriving just after the battle. His unit returned a week later and just missed another major fight, the New York City Draft Riots.[14]

One unit, the Forty-eighth New York Volunteers, had an unusually large number of clergymen. Led by the pastor of the Pacific Street Methodist Episcopal Church, West Point-educated Reverend Dr. James H. Perry, it became known as Perry's Saints. Their commander, a veteran of the Mexican War, felt an obligation to once more "take up my sword." Perry's presence resolved a dilemma for many religious parents. They wanted their offspring to fight for the Union but feared the amorality of army life. With Perry's presence they trusted that their sons would have a highly moral army experience. Although popular with his men, Perry's reputation suffered at the hands of the mean-spirited Eagle, when it snidely announced, "The parson did a good job to provoke this war so we are glad, for the honor of the cloth, to see that he did not shirk his responsibility."[15]

Camp Wyman, a part of Fort Hamilton, became the new home of Perry's Saints, and on July 24, 1861, two hundred men began their basic training. They left for the front on September 17, with nine hundred sixty-four soldiers, and fought in battles at the Crater, Fort Pulaski, Port Royal, Fort Wagner, and Fort Fisher. They suffered heavily in the Florida campaign, losing thirty-eight men at the battle of Olustee, and gained a second nickname, the "Die No Mores," after one of their favorite hymns. By the war's end the Forty-eighth had been in thirty-eight principal engagements and suffered a loss of eight hundred sixty-eight men over a three year period.[16]

Although the Forty-eighth Regiment had an abundance of religious leaders, many other outfits had none. This situation led to some comical moments and one story pointedly illustrated the great rivalry between New York and Brooklyn troops. Hearing that a New York outfit held no religious services, a zealous chaplain requested permission to perform the appropriate rites. The unit's colonel advised against it, claiming that all of his men were absolutely godless. The chaplain persisted, feeling that the Lord's work must be done "in season and out of season." He argued that he just prayed with a nearby Brooklyn regiment and -- but that was enough. The colonel ordered the regiment to fall in for divine worship, warning sternly that all smilers, coughers, or twitchers would be taken straight to the guardhouse. For a hour the chaplain preached his best for a silent, straight-backed congregation, and at the end asked if any men would step forward to profess the faith. No soldier moved. After waiting for several minutes, he admitted to being puzzled. He told the colonel that thirteen men had professed the faith in the Brooklyn unit. The colonel leaped to his feet. "Detail twenty men and have them baptized right now," he shouted to his adjutant, "My outfit is not going to let that damned Brooklyn regiment beat us at anything!"[17]

One of the war's more celebrated characters, Hiram Berdan, creator of the United States First Sharpshooter Regiment, lived in pre-war Flatlands, near Kimball and Coleman Streets, right off Flatbush Avenue. Berdan, a prolific inventor of range finders, cannon fuses, lifeboats, and trans-Atlantic cable-laying machinery, and one of America's foremost marksmen, wrote to President Abraham Lincoln suggesting a special outfit of expert shots who would wreak havoc on the enemy with their unique skills. Lincoln quickly gave his approval.[18]

Berdan's headquarters at 160 Montague Street advertised for able-bodied men of "good moral character and steady habits," who could make ten consecutive shots with a rifle averaging five inches from the center of a target at a distance of six hundred feet with a rest, or three hundred feet "off hand." Tryouts were held at the target grounds near 10th Avenue and 20th Street, and although the government provided ammunition, a rifle, and a proper rest, men could use their own weapons if they so chose. Berdan's select men, with new green uniforms and special telescopic rifle sights, participated in many battles, including the Peninsula, Antietam, Chancellorsville, Gettysburg, and Spotsylvania. Lieutenant George G. Hastings (3 Carroll Park) commanded the Sharpshooters for a brief period. Wounded at the battle of Chancellorsville, Virginia, he recuperated at his Brooklyn home.[19]

In November 1864 one of Berdan's many inventions, a repeating rifle, was tested in Flatbush. A large number of American and English officers watched as Berdan outshot two marksmen using other guns. Neither of his competitors could hit the target at two hundred yards, but Berdan scored on seven of twenty attempts, proving, he said, the superiority of his weapon.[20]

The highly contentious Berdan became enmeshed in several courts martial. His fellow officers accused him not only of behavior unbecoming a military officer, but also of cowardice. Although exculpated by various courts, he resigned on January 2, 1864, under circumstances that to this day remain a mystery. He died suddenly in Washington, D.C. in 1894 and was buried in Arlington National Cemetery.[21]

In an effort to stimulate enlistments, Brooklyn's common council appropriated seventy-five thousand dollars for volunteers' families. Privately, boot manufacturer Whitehouse and Pierce, and the Union Ferry Company furnished equipment to their employees who had joined the service. Situations were guaranteed upon return and the new soldier's families received the men's salaries for the duration of the war. In addition, members of the Kings County Medical Society resolved to treat the families of volunteers free of charge during the new soldier's absence.[22]

When the war began the government found its navy inadequately prepared and began chartering steamships for use as men-of-war until proper ones could be built. They also seized ferry boats, painted them black, armed them with heavy guns, and commissioned them. Men's cabins stored ammunition, cables and chains, while women's quarters became messrooms, officer's quarters, and bunks. In 1861 the government converted two New York and Brooklyn Ferry Company vessels into the gunboats <u>Commodore Perry</u> and <u>Commodore Barney</u>. The Union Ferry Company turned over the <u>Whitehall</u>, the <u>Wyandank</u>, the <u>Somerset</u>, the <u>Atlantic</u> and the <u>Ellen</u>, to the government for blockade duty, and as troop transports. The <u>Commodore Perry</u> saw action off the coast of both the Carolinas and Virginia and helped capture or destroy eleven Confederate vessels during the first three months of the war. Because of their open centers many ferries saw rebel shot pass right through them without causing any real damage.[23]

In August 1862 a peculiar incident occurred involving Brooklyn's medical community and their participation in the war. New York Mayor George Opdyke told Brooklyn

Postmaster George B. Lincoln of the government's need for volunteer surgeons to treat men wounded in the Second Battle of Bull Run. The mayor suggested that Lincoln convince some of Brooklyn's physicians to help. Lincoln persuaded ten doctors to volunteer, arranged their transportation to the capital, and returned home to 49 Cranberry Street to find his house filled with physicians, one of the largest gatherings ever of Brooklyn medical men. Twenty additional doctors left that evening for the south, but Lincoln remained puzzled for six months as to why they had all been there in the first place. Finally a neighbor solved the mystery. He had learned of Lincoln's quest and went directly to police headquarters, informing the authorities of the emergency. Each police precinct duly received a telegram ordering them to round up all of the area's physicians and have them rendezvous at Lincoln's house.[24]

Brooklyn played host to troops from various states as they headed for the front. On December 2, 1862, the Forty-Second Massachusetts Volunteers left camp at Union Course, near Cypress Hills Cemetery, expecting to move south. Finding their transport vessel unprepared for them, they spent the night in Brooklyn, receiving a hot supper from the Thirteenth New York State National Guard. Postmaster Lincoln fed ten of the company, provided a "good bed" for them and set a table in the morning for sixty. William Gilmore of 277 Hicks Street, served two hundred and fifty meals explaining that although he was too old to go to war he wanted to feed the boys. One man on Atlantic Avenue distributed coffee and cigars, and a widow gave supper to fifteen soldiers and then threw in lodgings and breakfast. "Bully for Brooklyn," concluded a soldier who described the hospitality of Brooklyn's citizens for the Barre, Massachusetts <u>Gazette</u>.[25]

The Fifth Massachusetts Regiment got a surprise during its stay in town. Inventor Elias Howe, Jr, who lived on Washington Avenue, presented a fully equipped stallion each to the unit's Colonel Lawrence and Lieutenant Colonel Greene.[26]

While awaiting orders, many out-of-state troops found themselves stationed in other Brooklyn locations. One soldier, sick with "the jaunders," wrote home from Camp Maine, in East New York, complaining of the sutler's overcharges, especiallly on tobacco, which rose to the unheard of price of one dollar a pound. At that rate, he reckoned that he would have to "nock off using the weed." He had never realized how debilitating jaundice could be and believed that the many Brooklyn "angels" saved his life by bringing oranges, lemons, cakes, jellies, and good cheer on a daily basis. One particular item, biscuits with butter and salt cod, tasted so good "it seemed like home."[27]

Brooklyn men joined the colors in droves and served in the infantry, engineers, cavalry, and navy in all of the eastern campaigns. No exact total of Brooklyn enlistees exists but estimates range between thirty thousand to forty thousand men, out of New York State's total of one hundred seventy-six thousand.[28]

The following is a partial list of outfits in which Brooklynites served:

First Engineers
Third Infantry
Fourth Cavalry
Fourth Heavy Artillery
Fifth Artillery (Jackson's)

Fifth Infantry (Duryee's Zouaves)

Fifth Cavalry (Bliss')

Fifth Independent Artillery (First Excelsiors)

Ninth Infantry (Hawkin's Zouaves, Zoo-Zoos)

Tenth Infantry (McChesney's Zouaves)

Eleventh Cavalry (Scott's Nine Hundred)

Thirteenth Cavalry

Thirteenth Artillery

Fifteenth Engineers (New York Sappers and Miners)

Sixteenth Artillery

Sixteenth Cavalry

Seventeenth New York Volunteers

Twentieth Infantry (Turner Rifles)

Twenty-third Cavalry

Thirty-sixth Infantry (Washington Volunteers)

Forty-Seventh Infantry (Washington Grays)

Fifty-fourth Infantry (Schwartze Jaeger, Barney Black Rifles)

Sixty-seventh Infantry (Beecher's Pets, Brooklyn Phalanx)

Seventieth Infantry (Steuben Guard)

Eighty-seventh Infantry (Brooklyn Rifles)

Eighty-eighth Infantry

Ninetieth Infantry (Hancock Guards, McLellan Chasseurs)

One Hundred and Second Infantry (Van Buren Light Infantry)

One Hundred Seventeenth Infantry

One Hundred Thirty-second Infantry

One Hundred Thirty-third Infantry (Metropolitan Guards)

One Hundred Thirty-seventh Infantry

One Hundred Thirty-ninth Infantry

One Hundred Fifty-fifth Infantry (Corcoran's Legion)
One Hundred Fifty-seventh Infantry
One Hundred Fifty-eighth Infantry (Spinola's Brigade)
One Hundred Fifty-ninth Infantry
One Hundred Sixty-third Infantry
One Hundred Sixty-fourth Infantry
One Hundred Sixty-fifth Infantry
One Hundred Seventieth Infantry
One Hundred Seventy-third Infantry (Fourth
Metropolitan Guard)
One Hundred Seventy-sixth Infantry (Old Ironsides)
Montezuma Rifles (Baxter Home Guard)[29]

[1] The History of the City of Brooklyn,(Stiles), vol.2, pp.438-440.
[2] Brooklyn Eagle, April 22,1861.
Brooklyn Evening Star, April 20,1861.
The History of the City of Brooklyn, (Stiles), Vol.2,
pp.438,439.
[3] Brooklyn Evening Star, April 22,1861.
[4] The History of the City of Brooklyn,(Stiles),vol.2,pp.440,447.
The History of the City of Brooklyn,(Howard), vol.2, p.148.
[5] Brooklyn Era, December 28,1861.
[6] Brooklyn Standard, June 15,1861.
[7] Brooklyn Eagle, June 6,1861.
[8] A History of the City of Brooklyn,(Ostrander),
Vol.2,pp.120,121.
[9] The History of the City of Brooklyn,(Stiles),vol.2, pp.438-
440,456-458.
A History of the City of Brooklyn,(Ostrander), Vol.2, p.126.

The History of the City of Brooklyn,(Howard), p.154.

Brooklyn and How It Got That Way, p.34.

New York in the War of the Rebellion, compiled by Frederick Phisterer, Albany,1890,pp.441,442.

The Red Legged Devils at Gettysburg, Colonel Charles G. Stevenson, The Magazine of History, no.13, New York, 1911, p.2.

Brooklyn Eagle, May 25,1864.

[10] Brooklyn Standard, July 6,1861.

The Civil War Dictionary, p.954.

[11] The History of the City of Brooklyn,(Stiles), vol.2, p.439, 456-458.

A History of the City of Brooklyn, (Ostrander),Vol. 2, pp.119,120,121.

[12] The History of the City of Brooklyn, (Stiles), vol.2,p.458.

The History of the City of Brooklyn, (Howard), p.149.

A History of the City of Brooklyn, (Ostrander), Vol.2, p.122.

[13] Swanberg, W.A.,Sickles,The Incredible(N.Y.,1956), p.116.

The Civil War Dictionary, p.350.

[14] Everdell, William R., and MacKay, Malcolm, Rowboats to Rapid Transit(Brooklyn, 1973), p.21.

[15] Nichols, James M., Perry's Saints(Boston,1886), pp.19,25.

Brooklyn Eagle, July 10,1861.

Palmer, Abraham, History of the 48th Regiment of New York in the War for the Union(Brooklyn,1885), p.3.

[16] History of the 48th Regiment, pp.28,29,32,113.

Brooklyn Eagle, August 1,1861.

[17] Goss, Warren Lee, Recollections of a Private(N.Y.,1890), p.256.

[18] Marcot, Roy, Hiram Berdan(Dallas, 1989), pp.17,20,23.

Map of the towns of Flatbush and Flatlands, 1858, N.Y.P.L.

Briggs, Charles, and Maverick, Augustus, <u>The Story of the Telegraph and a History of the Great Atlantic Cable</u>(N.Y.,1858), p.251.

[19] Brooklyn <u>Eagle</u>, August 15,1861.

Letter to the War Department from Lt. George Hastings, June 5,1863, author's collection.

<u>Civil War Dictionary</u>, p.736.

[20] New York <u>Times</u>, November 14,1864.

[21] <u>Hiram Berdan</u>, pp.67,98.

Death Certificate, Hiram Berdan, August 18,1893, author's collection.

[22] <u>The History of the City of Brooklyn</u> (Stiles), vol.2, pp.438-442.

<u>A History of the City of Brooklyn</u> (Ostrander), pp.118,119.

[23] <u>Rowboats to Rapid Transit</u>, p.21.

<u>Brooklyn's Eastern District</u>, p.24.

Minick, Rachel, <u>New York Ferryboats in the Union Navy</u>, New-York Historical Society Quarterly, vol. xlix, no.1, January 1965.

[24] <u>The History of the City of Brooklyn</u> (Stiles), Vol. 2, pp.448,449.

[25] <u>The History of the City of Brooklyn</u>(Stiles), vol.2., p.450.

[26] Brooklyn <u>Standard</u>, June 17,1861.

[27] Letter from Joel Winston to Kate, January 5,1862, author's collection.

[28] <u>A History of the City of Brooklyn (Ostrander)</u>, vol.2,p.127.

Brooklyn <u>Eagle</u>, November 14,1863.

[29] Brooklyn <u>Era</u>, December 12,1861.

<u>A History of the City of Brooklyn</u>,(Ostrander), vol.2.,pp.117,126,127.

<u>The Eagle and Brooklyn</u>, p.156.

<u>New York in the War of the Rebellion</u>, pp.441,442.

FORT HAMILTON AND FORT LAFAYETTE

Mindful of its defeat in the Battle of Long Island during the Revolutionary War, in 1807 the government built a fort in the southeastern corner of the town of New Utrecht on the very spot where the British army had landed in 1776. They named it for Alexander Hamilton, the first secretary of the treasury, and believed it would forever thwart any attempt by a foe to land forces on its shores.[1]

In 1840 Congress appropriated twenty thousand dollars to improve the fort's security and sent Captain Robert E. Lee to supervise the work. In the 1840's future Civil War generals John B. Sedgwick (Union), Thomas J.(Stonewall) Jackson (Confederate), and John Pemberton (Confederate), also served at Fort Hamilton, and Lee and Jackson became vestrymen at St. John's Episcopal Church, just a few blocks away. The Reverend Michael Schofield baptized Jackson at St. John's font on April 29, 1849, and Lee's name appears frequently in the vestry books. Known as "the Church of the Generals," St.John's has plaques adorning its walls commemorating these famous Confederate soldiers.[2]

On April 18, 1861, Fort Hamilton's personnel anxiously awaited the arrival of the north's first heroes, the defenders of Fort Sumter, South Carolina, who had surrendered to Confederate forces after the Civil War's first battle. Skeptical of reports that no casualties occurred during Sumter's ordeal, the worried families of Major Robert Anderson's men scanned the horizon daily looking for that special troop ship en route from the south. At last, the <u>Baltic</u>

entered the Narrows, flying Fort Sumter's torn banner at her bow. New York and Brooklyn went wild with joy while every vessel in the country's greatest harbor blew whistles or rang bells, and the men who drew the war's "first blood" heard cheers and huzzahs from admiring spectators on the shore. After being feted by New York City, Major Robert Anderson, the loyal Kentuckian, reported to Fort Hamilton with his men. He retold his experiences so often that he lost his voice and his next in command, Captain Abner Doubleday, spoke in his stead.[3]

In 1861, Fort Hamilton became the hub of artillery defense in the harbor, and its strength at times reached over one thousand men, including the Twelfth Infantry, under the command of General Harvey Brown. Brown would become an unsung hero during the famous Draft Riots of July 1863, leading his forces against maddened crowds during the height of the chaotic conditions in New York City.[4]

Fort Lafayette lay just one half mile northwest of Fort Hamilton. Its detractors called it the "Bastille of the North," in reference to the fact that it served as one of the federal government's more infamous prisons, housing upwards of two hundred rebels.[5]

The prisoners of Fort Lafayette included William Henry Fitzhugh Lee (Robert E. Lee's second son); fire-eater Roger Pryor, who goaded Virginia into seceding; Pierre Soule, former minister to Spain; and George Lamb Bickley, head of the "subversive" Knights of the Golden Cross, a dedicated organization of Copperheads. Young Lee's presence may have saved Federal soldiers captured near Richmond, Virginia, during the ill-fated 1864 Kilpatrick-Dahlgren Raid.

Papers discovered on the mortally wounded Colonel Ulric Dahlgren implied that any federal prisoners they could free would be encouraged to kill Confederate President Jefferson Davis. Some vindictive Confederate officials, particularly General Braxton Bragg, wanted to execute the captured raiders, but Secretary of War James Seddon suggested soliciting General Robert E. Lee's opinion first. Having a son in a Yankee jail proved motivation enough for Lee to recommend strongly against such drastic action.[6]

On April 27, 1861, fearful that Maryland would be lost to secessionists, President Lincoln ordered Lieutenant General Winfield Scott to announce the suspension of the writ of habeas corpus there.[7] From June through August 1861, federal officials placed a host of Maryland state legislators and all of the Baltimore board of police commissioners under arrest on suspicion of disloyalty. In three months President Lincoln had taken all suspected disunionists out of circulation, sending most of them to Fort Lafayette, and the crucial border state never seceded.[8]

The suspension of habeas corpus, however, would remain a thorn in the president's side throughout the war. Many loyal citizens regarded the writ as a prime protection against a sometimes overbearing government, one even the most loyal citizen could not always trust.[9] Beginning on August 11, 1861, and for four consecutive days, Kings County Sheriff Anthony Campbell arrived at Fort Hamilton and presented a writ of habeas corpus to Lieutenant Colonel Martin Burke, who commanded Fort Lafayette. Issued by Kings County Judge Samuel K. Garrison, it ordered the immediate release of prisoners Charles D. Howard, William

H. Gatchell, John G. Davis, and D. D. Hinks, all Baltimore police commissioners. Each day federal troops refused Sheriff Campbell entry, handing him a note from Lieutenant Colonel Martin Burke which read: "I deeply regret that, pending the existing political troubles, I cannot comply with the requisition of the Honorable Judge. By authority of Lieutenant General Winfield Scott." When Campbell brought the demurral back to Judge Garrison they pondered the idea of taking the aforementioned men by force, but concluded that this was not feasible since it would require the services of some five thousand to ten thousand men along with many pieces of field artillery. The writs continued to be issued through July 1863.[10]

Other Fort Lafayette residents included draft brokers, blockade runners, privateers, bounty jumpers, and political prisoners (Peace Democrats), all of whom appeared traitorous to a very nervous government. One short-term prisoner, Captain Robert Cobb Kennedy, had attempted, along with other Confederate agents, to burn New York City on November 25, 1864. He and his men had rented rooms in ten Manhattan hotels and then tried to set them ablaze with Greek fire, an incendiary device. In order to maintain secrecy, they closed all of their doors, thus limiting the very oxygen needed to encourage the flames. Much smoldering occurred but there were no great conflagrations. Apprehended and convicted, Kennedy was hung on Fort Lafayette's gallows on March 25, 1865.[11] A rebel named Thomas, known as the "French Lady," since he had tried to slip out of Baltimore in women's clothing, attempted to escape by strapping a number of corked canteens to his waist for buoyancy, jumping into the water, and swimming toward shore. The guards spotted him and a boat quickly caught the prisoner, restoring him once again to "government rations." Another enterprising young man served time at Fort Lafayette. Mathew F. Maury, a postman, specialized in delivering dispatches and letters between the north and the south for two dollars and fifty cents an ounce. When policemen seized him in Cleveland, Ohio, some of the missives impounded revealed that several prominent public citizens harbored pro-Confederate sympathies.[12]

At times the fort received unusual transients. Six deserters from the Confederate marine corps showed up in December 1861. The rebel leathernecks, all northerners, had been stranded in New Orleans at the outbreak of hostilities. Faced with the choice of starvation or imprisonment, or worse, they opted for enlistment in the Confederate forces, choosing the marines as the easiest branch from which they might desert. They did just that, in late 1861, surrendering to General Harvey Brown, then a colonel commanding Fort Pickens, Florida. The men, from Maine, Massachusetts, Wisconsin, and New York, were sent to Fort Lafayette for questioning, took a loyalty oath, and returned home.[13]

In 1863-64 some of the fort's literate prisoners wrote and circulated a clandestine newsletter called "The Right Flanker." Partly satirical, mostly sardonic, and highly critical of the diet of tough beef, dry bread, and bad coffee, the newsletter survived the war to be printed in London, England, in 1865, as "Fort La-Fay-Ette Life.[14]

The grousing notwithstanding, Fort Lafayette ranked as a pleasure island compared with other Civil War prisons such as the infamous Confederate site in Andersonville, Georgia, and Union jails in Elmira, New York and Fort Delaware, in the Delaware River. Many inmates admitted Fort Lafayette's cleanliness and relative comfort, and some even took the unusual step of proclaiming the fairness of their treatment in the New York <u>Times</u>.

"We the undersigned, this day released from imprisonment at Fort Lafayette state publicly that we received at the hands of Lt. Charles O. Wood, Ninth Inf. USA, commanding Ft. Lafayette, every civility, courtesy and kindness. We believe he would have made more provisions for our comfort had it been in his power to do so.

"Baltimore papers please copy.

"George N. Jones, A. N. Baker, R. W. Rasin, E. E. Cottrell, N. S. Reneau, J. M. Ogden, E.H. Jones, John Hagins, C. Ledwidge, Rutson Maury, Jr.

"Best wishes for his prosperity and happiness."[15]
Two generals languished in the "Bastille," one Confederate and one Union. Private Roger Pryor of Virginia, formerly a brigadier general in the Confederate army, had been captured near Petersburg, Virginia, in 1864. He shared a room with twelve others, slept on a straw mat, and cooked and kept the premises warm by burning coal in a small stove. Extra amenities, such as better food and liquor, appeared on a regular but illegal basis through sutlers or the bribing of a guard. Some of Pryor's companions carved rings or made caricatures of their commandant out of coal in an effort to avoid the devastating boredom of prison life. Pryor, former editor of the Richmond <u>Enquirer</u> and a well-known secessionist, failed to obtain a release for some time despite

repeated requests for leniency submitted by some of his northern friends to Secretary of War Edwin M. Stanton. The crusty former defense attorney reputedly said on seeing their pleas, "Release him? I'm going to hang the damned rebel." But word of Pryor's generosity toward captured Union troops during the battle of the Seven Days in 1862, when he paroled many instead of sending them south to prison camps, reached President Lincoln. The humanitarian chief executive ordered Pryor paroled to his home in Petersburg, Virginia, for the duration of the war.[16]

Ruined financially by the Confederacy's defeat, Pryor could no longer make a living at home and accepted a generous offer to write for the New York Daily News, owned by southern sympathizer Benjamin Wood. A crackerjack newspaper man in ante-bellum Virginia, Pryor felt comfortable with words and had popularized such expressions as "a house divided against itself" and "an irrepressible conflict", two phrases offered to the public by the well-known northern politicians Abraham Lincoln and William Seward. While supporting himself and his family through newspaper work Pryor studied law, and late in the fall of 1865 the New York state bar certified him. His talent for speaking helped in addressing a jury, and he became much sought after, serving as attorney for plaintiff Theodore Tilton in the infamous Henry Ward Beecher adultery trial in 1875. This trial gained him much praise and publicity from the press, and through the intercession of political leader and New York war hero Daniel Sickles, Pryor became first a judge of a lower court and then an associate justice on New York state's supreme court, thus completing the era's most astounding metamorphosis:

from Confederate general to respected New York state jurist.[17]

The Pryors lived at 127 Willow Street during his ascent toward judicial fame, and the general's wife, Sarah, spent a good deal of time assisting war orphans, many of southern birth. She especially enjoyed her Brooklyn Heights neighbors, maintaining that she had never met more hospitable people other than in the south. Many years later the Pryors moved to larger quarters in Manhattan where Sarah became involved with the Daughters of the American Revolution. She confessed to having had many problems with her new organization, not because she was a southerner and a former rebel, but because the Pryors had come from Brooklyn![18]

Roger Pryor, the last survivor of the firing on Fort Sumter, died in 1919. He is buried in the family plot in Princeton, New Jersey. [19]

The Union general, Charles P. Stone, although incarcerated for one hundred eighty-nine days never had charges pressed against him. No official explanation having ever been given, Stone could only guess that his imprisonment stemmed from his participation in the debacle of the Battle of Balls Bluff, Virginia, in October 1861, where Abraham Lincoln's close friend Colonel Edward D. Baker met his death. Many thought the newly assembled Joint Congressional Committee on the Conduct of the War had selected Stone as a scapegoat for this fiasco. Released on August 16, 1862, Stone served for a while in the Department of the Gulf but could not tolerate the strain of having a tarnished record and resigned from the army in 1864.[20]

A letter smuggled out of Fort Lafayette and printed in a Baltimore paper gave an excellent picture of prison life, complete with the standard gripes about lack of freedom, poor food, and tepid coffee:

"I know this will reach you despite the vigilance of our keepers. Given paper and writing materials and letters inspected by the commanding officer if not objectionable okay to mail but wrote twice and no word. Required to account for every inch of paper and deliver it up at night half written or empty and it is returned in the morning to finish. The fortification rises within twenty feet of the water on all sides and is about sixty feet in height forming a hollow square in which is a grass plot of thirty feet. Across this we are allowed to trample for two hours each day. At first okay but tire of the monotony and the weakness of our limbs induced by confinement and inferior diet. Makes us turn from exercise to repose. Our room is eighteen x twenty-four feet with a vaulted roof, the highest point only eight feet from the floor. Our bedsteads are four high posts on which there are two beds, one over the other, which with the two small or single bedsteads accomodate a party of six. We have straw ticks and are comparatively speaking comfortable enough in this particular. The room has three small windows in walls three feet thick. The ventilation through there, being from the sea, is quite fresh, making amends for the lowness of the ceiling, but it is unpleasant to be reminded of captivity by every passing vessel or pleasure boat glimpses of which we get through the peep holes. Mssrs Howard, Gatchell, Davis, Alvey, Lyon and Smith occupy a room similar to ours and share precisely the same privileges and miseries that we do. They take their meals from a sergeant in the garrison who supplies them with two meals a day for seven dollars a week which is exorbitant for what they receive, ham and eggs for breakfast and eggs and ham for dinner. They invited me to join but I declined because of the inability of my mess mates to do so. Their rations are dainty compared to ours. Breakfast is fat pork (no lean), four ounces of bread, tin cup of dark liquid called coffee, dinner four ounces of bread, one cup of pork soup, three ounces of overboiled indigestable lean beef and as much tepid water as we choose. Anything that might contribute to our comfort - newspapers - liquors- is forbidden. Mrs. ____ is kind in bringing us books and fresh vegetables but they were not passed on to us. We are denied every process of law and are shut out from the world in this bastille."[21]

In late January 1960, wreckers began to demolish the high, thick walls of the much-maligned bastion that guarded New York's harbor since the War of 1812. Fort Lafayette, which housed so many well-known rebels, blockade runners, "disloyal" Democrats, and the Baltimore police commissioners, would be gone forever. In its place would rise the east tower pier of the Verazzano Bridge, a permanent, if not quite appropriate memorial for one of the north's best known Civil War prisons.[22]

[1] Historic and Beautiful Brooklyn, printed by the Brooklyn Eagle, 1947.

[2] Ballard, Michael B., Pemberton(Jackson, Ms., 1991), p.26. Historic Fort Hamilton, Major Walter J. Gilbert, Our Army magazine, 1937, p.21.

[3] Brooklyn Eagle, April 18, 1861. Swanberg, W.A., First Blood(N.Y., 1957), pp.330,331.

[4] History of Fort Hamilton and Vicinity,1654-1942, United

States Army publication, Fort Hamilton archives, undated, p.14.

[5] Brooklyn <u>Standard</u>, September 18,1861.

<u>The Man Who Tried to Burn New York</u>, pp.199-201,209.

Bergin, Tunis, <u>The History of the Town of New Utrecht</u>(N.Y.,1884), p.9.

[6] Hallock, Judith L., <u>Braxton Bragg and Confederate Defeat</u>(Tuscaloosa, Ala.,1991), 2 vol., vol.2, p.170.

<u>The Civil War Dictionary</u>, p.478.

<u>The Man Who Tried to Burn New York</u>, p.209.

<u>Historic and Beautiful Brooklyn</u>.

[7] Latin for "you should have the body." <u>Habeas corpus</u> is a writ issued to bring a person before a court or judge in order to release that person from unlawful restraint or detention.

[8] <u>Official Records, War of the Rebellion</u>, Series II, Vol.I, <u>The Maryland Arrests</u>.

The slave states of Kansas, Missouri, Kentucky, Maryland, and Delaware did not secede.

[9] McPherson, James M., <u>Battle Cry of Freedom</u>(N.Y., Oxford,1988),pp.288,289,592.

[10] New York <u>Times</u>. August 11, 1861.

[11] <u>The Civil War and New York City</u>, pp.287-290.

<u>The Man Who Tried To Burn New York</u>, p.231.

[12] New York <u>Times</u>, September 11,1861, April 23,1862.

[13] Donnelly, Ralph W., <u>The Confederate States Marine Corps: The Rebel Leathernecks</u>(Shippensburg, Pa., 1989), p.28.

[14] <u>Fort La-Fay-Ette Life</u>, anonymous, 1866, N.Y.P.L.

[15] <u>The Man Who Tried To Burn New York</u>, p.209.

New York <u>Times</u>, February 2,1862.

[16] Holtzman, Robert, <u>Adapt or Perish</u>(Hamden, Ct.,1976), pp.67,68,70,76,78,80,81.

[17] As a Confederate general Roger Pryor commanded a brigade during the battles of Williamsburg and Seven Pines in 1862, but resigned on August 18, 1863. He then enlisted as a private in the cavalry corps. This seems to be the only instance during the Civil War where a soldier reduced his own rank from brigadier general to private.
Adapt or Perish, pp.21,89,90,103,129,131.

[18] Adapt or Perish, p.115.
New York Times, June 11,14,1891.

[19] Adapt or Perish, p.156.
The Civil War Dictionary, p.674.

[20] The Civil War Dictionary, p.800.

[21] Brooklyn Eagle, August 15,1861.

[22] New York Times, February 3,1960.

THE DRAFT AND THE DRAFT RIOTS

Chances for a southern victory seemed slim in July 1863. Confederate General John Pemberton had surrendered his thirty thousand man army to Union General Ulysses S. Grant at Vicksburg, Mississippi, and the invasion of the formidable rebel Army of Northern Virginia pressed no further than Gettysburg, Pennsylvania. In the north, however, patriotic fervor had declined. The chilling realities of long casualty lists and maimed veterans caused enlistments to taper off while desertions became commonplace. This combination forced the government to introduce conscription in an effort to raise more troops, a step the Confederates had taken in April, 1862.[1]

Congress passed the draft law on March 3, 1863, and a month later President Lincoln ordered a levy of three hundred thousand men to be inducted in July. All males between twenty and thirty-five, and all unmarried men between thirty-five and forty-five, would be subject to conscription. Government agents had obtained lists of those eligible through house-to-house canvassing.[2]

The new regulations permitted anyone to furnish an acceptable substitute or to pay to the commissioner of internal revenue in his congressional district a three hundred dollar commutation fee which would exempt him from that particular draft call. John Stillwell, of Kings County's ninth ward, was one who took advantage of the law by providing someone to serve for him. His certificate of non-liability stated that he "was not properly subject to do military service as required by

145

the federal government as he had furnished an acceptable substitute."[3] Since supplying a substitute carried no stigma, worthies like Theodore Roosevelt, Sr.[4] and future president Grover Cleveland used this device to avoid serving. Anyone rich enough to pay a substitute or the commutation fee could stay home, while the average male citizen, who earned less than three hundred dollars yearly, would be marched off to war. This blatantly unfair arrangement created deep currents of resentment on the part of the urban poor, especially the Irish.[5]

One might also be excused from the draft if suffering from one of the fifty-one ailments calling for deferment. These ranged from irreducible dislocation of the elbow to manifest imbecility. Also, an exemption would be granted to the only son of a widow or aged parent, or to the father of a motherless child.[6]

The Standard held some prominent men in contempt for providing substitutes. "Abolitionist Theodore Tilton, champion of the Union, declined the invitation of the provost marshall to shoulder arms," the paper chided. "So far as fighting material is concerned, the arrangement is best for the efficiency of the service. These rampant abolitionists are all poor, white-livered creatures and would faint away at the smell of a gun, though terribly truculent with tongue and pen." They lauded, however, the Reverend A. A. Willitts who was anxious to meet the enemy "with a sword in one hand and the Constitution in the other." The minister offered himself as a substitute as he had not been called up.[7]

Others had a different attitude. One conversation reportedly ran as follows:

Mr. Castor, what do you think of the draft?

Let it come. I'm ready. If I'm drafted I shall go.

Where to, Mr. Castor?

Canada![8]

Another way to avoid the service, one newspaper volunteered with tongue in cheek, was to disobey the law. Under the election laws a man who made a bet on the election lost his right to vote. Since a man could be drafted only where he was entitled to vote, he could avoid conscription by betting illegally. Especially, the paper added, if the bet was that Ben Prince[9] would be elected mayor of Brooklyn.[10]

Kings County had a quota of three thousand seventy-five men, while New York had twelve thousand five hundred, Queens County thirteen hundred, Suffolk County seven hundred, and Richmond County four hundred. Out of Kings County's eligible pool of men totaling twenty-one thousand five hundred fifty-three, almost fifteen per cent could be drafted. The names of each eligible man was written on a six-inch by one-inch piece of paper, rolled up, and secured by an rubber band. The slips were then placed in a revolving box and drawn, one by one, by a blindfolded man.[11] The New York <u>Times</u> believed this method of choosing men by lottery a good one. Since everyone ran the same risk, they maintained, the draft "will fall as noiselessly as the snow flake." This judgment, rendered the day prior to the great Draft Riots, proved highly unrealistic.[12]

New York's provost marshal drew the first names for the draft on Saturday, July 11, 1863, and newspapers printed the lists the following day, a Sunday, when those most affected by conscription were at home. This turned out to be a grave mistake as it gave the workers, particularly the Irish, time to ponder the consequences of entering the army to fight and perhaps to die in a war they wanted no part of, being fought for a portion of the population that might one day displace them at their jobs. Had the draft lists been published on a working day, the laborers would have been scattered at different sites, unable to gather for weighty discussions. But on this particular Sabbath heated consultations took place, and long-festering resentments toward the rich, who could buy their way out, and toward the blacks, whom they felt caused the whole war, surfaced in angry talk. Irish laborers recognized a strong similarity to England's oppression of their people and on Monday many failed to report to work. They united into groups, and these groups soon evolved into mobs, and these mobs let loose a reign of terror that New York City had not seen in its entire existence. Led by boiling-mad Irish workers and gathering more forces -- men, women, children -- as they marched, they threw rocks and bricks at whatever decent-looking homes they found, set fires, destroyed a Negro church and the Colored Orphan Asylum on 44th Street, beat anyone who got in their way, and lynched several blacks. They terrorized entire neighborhoods, broke into the draft office, destroyed all of the records, and attacked and demolished the provost marshal's home. They became roaring drunk on stolen liquor, ransacked firearms shops and the armory at 2nd Avenue and 21st Street, and when they encountered the police they drove them back with a hail of bullets, bricks, and rocks. At each corner city forces attempted to halt the rampage, and a pitched battle ensued. The police, sometimes greatly outnumbered, fought back with their locusts (truncheons), pistols and whatever weapons came to hand. The mob, numbering thousands, menaced anyone they thought was wealthy, black, or connected with the hated conscription act, and threatened any worker who would not join them. As always, they attracted hundreds of adventurers and outright thugs who took advantage of the chaos to loot and maim.[13]

The riots caused great anxiety in Brooklyn lest dockworkers should decide to cross the East River to participate. Although some certainly did, the vast majority of Brooklyn's citizens remained peaceful, the police intervening in the few incidents of overt hostility towards blacks.[14]

The Metropolitan Police Force, controlled by New York State, included ten Brooklyn police precincts. On Monday, July 13, New York headquarters directed Brooklyn's Inspector John S. Folk to ready his reserves, and at 5:00 p.m. New York Police Commissioner John Bergen asked for the entire force if Folk thought Brooklyn would remain quiet. Folk decided that it would, and headed with more than two hundred men to Manhattan's Mulberry Street headquarters. At 8:00 p.m., hearing that rioters threatened the Tribune building, New York's Inspector Carpenter led his New York/ Brooklyn contingent to the trouble spot. In a violent clash near Printing House Square the police emerged victorious. Folk and his men then marched off to the Brooklyn ferries amidst cheers from their New York compatriots.[15]

On July 14 Brooklyn's provost marshals S. B. Gregory and Samuel Maddox moved all of their lists and enrollment papers to a safe place, and Fire Department Chief Engineer John Cunningham ordered all firemen to remain on duty throughout the emergency. Officials hustled off the state arsenal's inventory, consisting of large and small guns, field artillery, and five thousand stacks of arms, to a remote location. The heavily protected Navy Yard had thirteen pound cannons on the Flushing Avenue side and thirty-two pounders at the main gate. All police vessels remained on the alert and Mayor Kalbfleisch remained at City Hall throughout the night with a one-hundred man police reserve.[16]

A number of men, women, and children looted the Brooks Brothers clothing store on Catherine Street in Manhattan, then fled to Brooklyn on the ferry. Meeting them at the slip, Forty-second Precinct police arrested the lot. Brooklynites James Lee, Richard Balensburg, and Patrick Dougherty had gone to New York to participate in the riots. Dougherty was killed, and Lee and Balensburg were charged with stealing. In a time-honored tradition, Lee was offered a choice of enlisting in the army or going to jail. He opted to join the colors. The police eventually dropped the charges against Balensberg, but held Elizabeth Archer, fifteen-year-old Anthony Smith, and Thomas Smith. Convicted and sentenced to six months, Miss Archer went to jail while the youth gained release because of his age. The case against Thomas Smith could not be proved and he, too, went free. The police also collared William Wood and William Hartley who had extorted twenty-five cents from a storekeeper on Columbia Street. Boasting that they were among the New York rioters, they had threatened to smash the store if not paid off. Both were remanded to the Grand Jury for further action.[17]

On Wednesday, July 15, in the only major incident in

Brooklyn, an angry mob of two hundred people, including some disgruntled ex-employees, set fire to two grain elevators in the Atlantic Avenue Basin. One building, worth eighty thousand dollars and the other, a floating elevator worth twenty-five thousand dollars, went up in flames. Despite harassment, firemen managed to extinguish the conflagration and the crowds dispersed after a short encounter with the police. Sheriff Anthony F. Campbell recommended that citizens organize into a posse comitatis for protection and Mayor Kalbfleisch issued an address congratulating his fellow citizens on their restraint.[18]

In the midst of the rioting some intrepid Brooklynites met at Gothic Hall on Adams Street to volunteer their services in suppressing the violence. The mob controlled so much of Manhattan that after crossing the river by ferry each man had to proceed individually to Major General Edward Sandford, commander of the state armory at 7th Avenue and 35th Street. The building, a prime target for the rioters, contained an immense amount of arms and ammunition. The city, having been stripped of its military forces for the battle of Gettysburg, had only the Third Cavalry, along with parts of other companies to protect the building. As the Brooklyn men appeared one by one they were assigned to guard prisoners. Several attacks met stiff resistance and the thin line of defense held, keeping the mob at bay. Unhappilly, the volunteers' names never became public.[19]

Back in Brooklyn, several black women fled to the Forty-second Precinct with reports of crowds threatening their lives. But in Greene Lane, Stewart's Alley, and Talman Street the police found only a group of small boys who threw rocks and whooped it up. Some toughs chased a black sailor along Hudson Street, but a number of whites interceded and the man escaped into the Navy Yard. Pink Row near Canton Street, normally bustling with people, appeared empty, its black population having disappeared. On July 16 word came that a crowd on East Warren Street threatened a black man. Captain George R. Rhodes and Sergeant John Matthews of the Forty-third Precinct entered the building at 185 Warren Street and found the potential victim armed with a revolver. The police took him and several women and children to the station for protection.[20]

The black community of Weeksville learned that Jamaica, Long Island, rioters were heading their way. Sworn in as deputy sheriffs, blacks armed themselves to protect their homes, a scant four miles from the East River ferries. Weeksville and its neighbor Carrville became a haven for blacks fleeing New York and Brooklyn. Overnight, strangers clogged the roads to Flatbush, Flatlands, and New Brooklyn, (north of Weeksville's Hunterfly Road), as refugees sought shelter and safety. By arming themselves and throwing out pickets for advance warning, Weeksville and Carrville blacks escaped the fate of some of their New York brethren.[21]

Peter W. Ray of 272 South 4th Street, the first black physician accepted by the Kings County Medical society, owned a pharmacy in lower Manhattan. His Irish neighbors protected his store during the riots, testifying to his popularity, but the mob in New York chased teamster John Camble to the docks where he dove into the East River and swam to Williamsburg and safety.[22]

After three days of violence the police finally gained

the upper hand. Federal troops arrived, battle-hardened veterans from the Army of the Potomac who had just repelled the Confederate invasion of Pennsylvania at Gettysburg. Calm finally prevailed, but at the cost of some one hundred fifteen lives and over one million dollars in damages. Original estimates had ranged as high as one thousand dead, and the exact figure is still in dispute but recent scholarship, including a detailed look at burial records, funerals, and names suddenly missing from the city directory determined that the closest figure was near the hundred mark.[23]

Fort Hamilton had supplied many of the troops who helped contain the rioting. Brigadier General Harvey Brown had ordered Captain H. H. Putnam and his Twelfth United States Infantry, Company F, and Captain George Chappell's First Battalion of Artillery to New York to augment the police force. In his post-riot report, Putnam lauded his officers and men who, without exception, performed like veterans, especially Sergeant Patrick Roach who had charge of the skirmishers. Captain Walter S. Franklin also praised his men for their coolness despite the fatigue caused by their long marches over stone pavements in the July heat. He gave special commendation to Corporal Raymond, who with eight of his men guarded New York Mayor Opdyke's home. Throughout the riot, he added, his company never had more than one hundred twenty men.[24]

In the riot's aftermath, the common council decided to aid in exempting firemen and certain militia men from military service. Brooklyn's board of supervisors voted to borrow two hundred fifty thousand dollars for payments of three hundred dollar bounties for every substitute enlisted in place of any drafted man. They would pay these amounts very cautiously, as a new industry had sprung up, which in the working man's vernacular became known as "lapin' the bounty," or bounty jumping.[25]

Many citizens claimed damage during the riots and demanded compensation. One woman asked for five dollars for the loss of a hog, and another asked for five thousand dollars for the loss of her husband. The former, the Standard facetiously declared, stood the best chance of getting her claim allowed, as pork has a market value, but men have none, except under the conscription act, which only estimates a live specimen at three hundred dollars.[26]

Fortunately for Brooklyn, Kings County filled its draft quota in September 1864, and while thousands of potential conscripts felt relief, brokers saw their profits cut off. Draft-age men indulged in much second guessing. Those who had furnished substitutes wished that they had saved their money, and substitutes holding back for higher prices felt that they had made a mistake. The navy took credit for this change in the draft status, albeit indirectly, as the efforts of aldermen and supervisors to have previous naval enlistments credited to Brooklyn finally proved fruitful, leaving an excess of seventy-one against any future draft calls as of February 24, 1865.[27]

New York was not alone in its experience with the Draft Riots. Confrontations also took place in Rutland, Vermont, Portsmouth, New Hampshire, and Wooster, Ohio. These, however, proved minor compared with the destruction wrought by outraged workers in Manhattan. President Lincoln's need for new troops, however, overroad any fear concerning future turmoil, and the draft commenced once again in New York on August 17. Although federal troops stood ready to quell any new disturbances none occurred and the draft resumed, this time in a peaceful manner.[28]

[1] The Civil War Dictionary, pp.75,172.
Costello, Augustine E., Our Police Protectors History of the New York Police(N.Y., 1885), 2 vol., vol.1, p.161.

[2] Our Police Protectors, vol.1, p.161.
Bernstein, Iver,The New York City Draft Riots(New York, 1990),p.8.

[3] Stillwell papers, manuscript collection, N.Y.P.L.

[4] President Theodore Roosevelt's father.

[5] Brooklyn Eagle, July 10, 1863.
Headley, Joel T., The Great Riots of New York 1712-1873(N.Y., 1873), p.139.

[6] New York Times, July 12,1863.
Brooklyn Eagle, July 10,1863.

[7] Brooklyn Standard, September 3,5,12,1863.

[8] Brooklyn Daily Union, August 1,1863.

[9] Ben Prince gained the least votes in the mayoral election of 1862.

[10] Brooklyn Standard, August 29,1863.

[11] Brooklyn Standard, August 29, 1863. The History of the City of Brooklyn(Stiles), vol.2, p.453.New York Times, July 12,1863.

[12] Ibid., July 11,1863.

[13] The History of the City of Brooklyn (Stiles), Vol.2,pp.451-453.
The Great Riots of New York, pp.149,155,169-172.
Our Police Protectors, Vol.1, pp. 164-200.
The Civil War and New York City, pp.198,199.

[14] The History of the City of Brooklyn,(Stiles), vol.2, p.451-453.

[15] The History of the City of Brooklyn,(Stiles), vol.2, p.451-453.
Our Police Protectors, pp.173-175,180.

[16] The History of the City of Brooklyn,(Stiles), vol.2, p.451-453.
Our Police Protectors, vol.1, pp.173-175,180.

[17] The History of the City of Brooklyn,(Stiles), vol.2, p.451-453.
Brooklyn Eagle, July 14,1863.
New York Times, July 16,1863.

[18] The History of the City of Brooklyn,(Stiles), vol.2, p.451-453.
Brooklyn Standard, July 11,1863.
A History of the City of Brooklyn,(Ostrander), vol.2, p.121.

[19] The History of the City of Brooklyn,(Stiles), vol.2, p.451-453.

[20] Brooklyn Eagle, July 14,1863.

[21] The Negro's Civil War, pp.72,73.
Anti-Negro Riots in the North,1863, edited by William L.
Katz, New York, 1969, pp.25,30.
Weeksville Curriculum Unit, pp.10,11.
People of Brooklyn, p.19.
Weeksville, Then and Now, p.20.

[22] Brooklyn and How It Got That Way, p.40.
Murals, Muse Museum, Lincoln Place and Bedford Avenue,
Brooklyn.
A Ghetto Grows in Brooklyn, p.23.

[23] The History of the City of Brooklyn (Stiles), Vol.2, pp.451-453.
The Civil War and New York City, pp.208,209.

[24] The Great Riots of New York, pp.264,265,371.

[25] Brooklyn Standard, August 22,1863.
The Civil War Dictionary, p.75.
A History of the City of Brooklyn,(Howard), p.149.

Bounty jumping referred to the taking of bounty money,
then deserting and enlisting again in another location
for another bounty. This practice continued throughout the war.

[26] Brooklyn <u>Standard</u>, August 16, 1863.

[27] <u>The History of the City of Brooklyn</u>(Stiles), vol. 2, pp.474, 475.

[28] The <u>Civil War Dictionary</u>, p.246.

<u>The Civil War and New York City</u>, p.213.

THE SANITARY FAIR OF 1864

As the precursor of the Red Cross and the U.S.O. the Sanitary Commission performed invaluable work for Union soldiers during the Civil War. It cared for the sick and wounded, provided morale-boosting services, obtained financial help, pensions and pay, and inspected camp and field hospitals to insure decent accomodations. It also maintained hospital directories which enabled visiting relatives and friends to find sick or wounded servicemen more readily.[1]

In 1864 Brooklyn decided to raise money to aid the commission's work. The city's Sanitary Fair soon took shape through the efforts of one hundred thirty prominent citizens of the War Fund Committee of Brooklyn and Kings County, and women from fifty churches that comprised the Women's Relief Association of the City of Brooklyn. On opening day, Washington's birthday, February 22, the city's military forces marched past the Academy of Music on Montague Street, reviewed by Abbot Low, Frederic Farley, James H. Frothingham, and Abraham R. Frothingham, the fair's officers.[2]

Creating a European-type market fair had been discussed at the Sanitary Aid Society long before the Chicago, Cincinnati, and Boston fairs took place. Brooklynites chafed as the projected New York Fair, in which Brooklyn would participate, seemed delayed until April, so the impatient locals decided to do it on their own. Hoping to raise one hundred thousand dollars, the Society named twenty men to work with the Relief Association Women. When they elected Abbot Low the fair president he immediately pledged twenty-five hundred dollars. Hearing this, his brother-in-law, George B. Archer, gave one thousand dollars, and in short order other donations brought in a surprising twenty-five thousand dollars before the fair even got off the ground.[3]

Montague Street, site of the Academy of Music, became the fair's headquarters. Workmen erected a two-story restaurant called Knickerbocker Hall and joined it by a covered bridge to the Hall of Manufacturers and the New England Kitchen. The spacious Taylor home at Montague and Clinton Streets became the Museum of Arts, Relics and Curiosities, and the home of Drum-Beat, the fair's daily newspaper.[4]

Most of the sales booths of the Great Central Bazaar could be found in the Academy of Music, where boards set over the great auditorium created an eleven thousand square foot emporium. While a large bald eagle, grasping the national shield, held forth on invisible wires high above the sales floor, patriotic decorations hung everywhere, with gas-jets proclaiming "In Union Is Strength." Near the stage wall stood a large painting of a Sanitary Commission field hospital, and a nearby tent offered not only the newest war photos and souvenirs but also featured wounded soldiers attended by Sanitary Commission workers. One particular crowd favorite, the "Skating Pond," was the work of Helen Anthony of the First Universalist Church. Her optical illusion created by mirrors showed an ice pond filled with smartly dressed skaters. For atmosphere, many families lent priceless paintings, including Henry E. Pierrepont's Gilbert Stuart portrait of George Washington.[5]

And the food! Hundreds contributed home-made

products for sale, while the Knickerbocker Hall restaurant featured green turtle soup (thirty-five cents), brook trout (fifty cents), and striped bass (twenty cents), all of which netted almost twenty-four thousand dollars.[6]

In the hall of curiosities sat Governor John Bradford's table, a century old; a sword presented to Light Horse Harry Lee, Revolutionary War hero and father of Confederate General Robert E. Lee; a clock that had been damaged by British bullets in 1778; a chair that had been buried lest the British should sit on it; and Patrick Henry's rifle.[7]

On March 11, after a calico ball, the festivities ended. The fair's success went far beyond the most optimistic forecasts. At closing the treasurer reported twice the income expected and auctions earned even more money as boards from temporary buildings and the vast auditorium were sold to the highest bidder. The Sanitary Commission, highly impressed, wrote that Brooklyn's contribution of four hundred thousand dollars "was by far the largest amount ever put into our treasury at one time by any community."[8] A huge broom had earlier been sent from Cincinnati with the message: "Greetings. We have swept up two hundred forty thousand dollars, Brooklyn, beat this if you can." After totaling up all their receipts Brooklyn proudly responded: "Brooklyn sees the two hundred forty and goes one hundred fifty better."[9]

Perhaps <u>Drum Beat</u> summed it up best with this poem:

Come hither, come hither
For I vow and declare
You ne'er saw such sights
As you'll see at our fair.
For use or for fancy,

Admiration or wear,

We've everything here,

Will you come to the Fair?

Will you have a bride's trousseau,

My tender young miss?

To get one, I'm sure,

There's no place like this,

Or perhaps you're in quest

Of something more rare,

You cannot but find it,

If you'll come to the Fair.[10]

Brooklyn had every reason to be delighted with the fair and the money it raised for such a worthy cause. In addition, the city had "stolen a march" on New York and that pleased it very much, too.

[1] The Civil War Dictionary, p.720.

Brooklyn Standard, February 22,1864.

Drum Beat, February 22,1864.

[2] The History of the City of Brooklyn,(Stiles), vol.2, pp.459-467.

New York Times, February 23,1864.

The History of the First Unitarian Church, pp.61-65.

[3] The History of the City of Brooklyn,(Stiles), vol.2, pp.459-467.

The History of the First Unitarian Church, pp.61-65.

[4] The History of the City of Brooklyn,(Stiles), vol.2, pp.459-467.

New York Times, February 23,1864.

Brooklyn Daily Union, February 22,1864.

Brooklyn Standard, February 22,1864.

[5] The History of the City of Brooklyn,(Stiles), vol.2, pp.459-467.

Brooklyn Daily Times, February 23,1864.

Brooklyn <u>Standard</u>, February 23,1864.

New York <u>Times</u>, February 23,1864.

[6] Brooklyn Daily <u>Union</u>, February 22,1864.

[7] <u>Ibid</u>., February 23,1864.

[8] <u>The History of the First Universalist Church</u>, pp.61-65.

[9] <u>The History of the City of Brooklyn</u>,(Stiles), vol.2, pp.459-467. The broom then passed to New York which collected $1,340,000 from its Sanitary Fair.

[10] Brooklyn <u>City News</u>, February 23,1864.

THE WAR ENDS

On April 14, 1865, the federal government held special flag-restoring services at Fort Sumter, South Carolina. Brooklyn's two most prominent clergymen, Henry Ward Beecher and Richard S. Storrs, attended along with Mayor Alfred Wood. The capture of Charleston, South Carolina, gave the federals the opportunity to raise once again the very flag that had flown there in April 1861. Major Robert Anderson, the fort's former commander, had the honor of raising the colors, and after Beecher delivered the oration, Dr. Storrs conducted services. The attendees included Senator Henry Wilson and abolitionist William Lloyd Garrison, who had had a price on his head in Charleston in ante-bellum days.[1]

The guests heard Beecher deliver one of the eloquent speeches for which he was famous. A large party of Brooklynites also attended the ceremonies, arriving on the chartered steamship Oceana. As the flag rose above Sumter's battered walls, every harbor battery that had fired upon it four years earlier saluted it again, this time with a more friendly roar of its cannons.[2]

On hearing of General Lee's surrender on April 10, 1865, Brooklyn rejoiced, but the euphoria vanished quickly with word of President Lincoln's assassination. Alderman D.D. Whitney, as acting mayor while Mayor Wood was at Fort Sumter, issued a proclamation directing flags to be displayed at half-mast, and bells tolled from noon until 1 p.m. All public offices, theaters, and amusement areas were closed and everywhere a sense of despair permeated the city.[3]

Brooklyn's municipal and county authorities, public bodies, military loyal leagues, and citizens joined in President Lincoln's funeral cortege, when it wended its way along New York City's streets on April 26, 1865.[4]

Thus ended Brooklyn's role during the Civil War.

[1] A History of the City of Brooklyn,(Ostrander),Vol.2,p.125. Henry Ward Beecher, An American Portrait, p.198.

[2] Ibid.

[3] History of the City of Brooklyn(Ostrander), Vol.2,p.477.

[4] The Civil War and New York City, p.307.

EPILOGUE

No doubt, the building of the <u>Monitor</u> stands out as Brooklyn's greatest contribution to the war effort. The vessel's emergence at Hampton Roads and its stand-off battle with the <u>Merrimac</u> perhaps altered the war's outcome. Its importance cannot be exaggerated. The <u>Merrimac</u> had already put the thirty-gun <u>Cumberland</u> and the fifty-gun <u>Congress</u> out of commission, their fire having bounced harmlessly off the ironclad's sides. Many feared the <u>Merrimac</u> would destroy the north's entire wooden fleet and bombard the Capitol from the Potomac River, both with impunity. The shock of Washington being fired on would have been incalculable and the ruination of the wooden fleet would have negated the blockade which became increasingly effective as the war continued. So Brooklyn's building of the <u>Monitor</u> was paramount to the Union's cause.

In addition, the Navy Yard built fourteen ships that saw action, converted scores of civilian vessels into men-of-war or troop carriers, and repaired countless more. Robert Squibb's pharmaceutical company accounted for eight per cent of all federal medicinal purchases and his ether made its way clandestinely through the lines, easing the suffering of many wounded Confederate soldiers. The company's panniers saved countless Union lives as they became indispensable items for every army surgeon.

The city's amazing success with its 1864 Sanitary Fair revealed a surprising talent for raising funds for a worthy cause. Most important, it reflected Brooklyn's first great act of self-assertion. Even then Brooklyn felt the need to prove itself equal to New York City.

During New York's Draft Riots Brooklyn remained largely untouched. Troops from Fort Hamilton and the city's police came to the aid of New York's beleagured forces, and Weeksville and Carrville provided shelter and food to many blacks fleeing Manhattan. Brooklyn's lack of participation in the actual rioting speaks volumes about its less volatile, law-abiding citizenry. For once, being "outdone" by New York proved a blessing.

The recalcitrance of the Brooklyn <u>Eagle</u> must astonish past readers. Its criticism of the Union's role in the war caused it great trouble and its candor provoked a government that saw traitors under every bed. But the <u>Eagle</u>, showing the resiliency that would enable it to last another ninety years, changed its editor and its policies. Its doubtful loyalty comes as a shock to those of us who read it daily in our youthful days of the 1940's and 1950's.

That the infamous John Wilkes Booth played twice at the Brooklyn Academy of Music adds a touch of spice to the history of Brooklyn's life during the Civil War and knowing of the existence of Master Eddie, the female impersonator, casts a revealing light on the entertainment tastes and tolerances of that day.

Brooklyn built the <u>Monitor</u>, supplied the Union armies with large quantities of medicines, provided thousands of soldiers and sailors who helped save the Union, and played host to the great Brooklyn Navy Yard. During the Civil War era, with the obvious exceptions of Washington, D.C. and Richmond, Virginia, the respective capitals of the opposing forces, more fascinating things occurred in Brooklyn and more interesting people visited or lived in Brooklyn than in any other city in the country. It deserves a better fate than relegation to the footnotes of American or New York City history. During the Civil War era Brooklyn's unique accomplishments earned it the right to be called one of America's most distinguished cities.

BIBLIOGRAPHY

Abelow, Samuel P, History of Brooklyn Jewry(Brooklyn, N.Y., 1937.)

Allen, Gay Wilson, The Solitary Singer(N.Y.,1967).

Anti-Negro Riots in the North, 1863, edited by William L. Katz (New York, 1969).

Armbruster, Eugene, Brooklyn's Eastern District(Brooklyn, N.Y., 1942).

Ballard, Michael B., Pemberton(Jackson, Ms., 1991)

Battles and Leaders, edited by Robert U. Johnson and Clarence Buel(New York, 1884-1887).

Baxter, James P. 3rd, The Introduction of the Ironclad Warship(Hamden,Ct.,1968)

Bergen, Tunis, History of the Town of New Utrecht(Brooklyn, 1884).

Bernstein, Ivor, New York City Draft Riots(New York 1990).

Bishop, Joseph, and Bishop, Farnham, George Goethals, Genius of the Panama Canal(New York, 1930).

The Black Military Experience, edited by Ira Berlin, (New York 1982).

Blochman, Lawrence C., Dr. Squibb(New York, 1958).

Boatner, Mark III, The Civil War Dictionary(New York, 1959).

The Boroughs of Brooklyn and Queens, Counties of Nassau and Suffolk, Long Island, N.Y. 1609-1924, edited by Henry Isham Hazelton, (New York, 1925), 7 vol.

Braden, Waldo W., Abraham Lincoln, Public Speaker(L.S.U.,1988)

Brandt, Nat, The Man Who Tried To Burn New York(Syracuse, 1986).

Briggs, Charles F. and Maverick, Augustus, The Story of the Telegraph and a History of the Great Atlantic Cable(N.Y.,1858).

Callender, James H., Yesterdays on Brooklyn Heights(N.Y., 1927).

Carpenter, George R., Walt Whitman(New York, 1909).

Church, William C., The Life of John Ericsson(N.Y., 1911).

Clark, Clifford E, Henry Ward Beecher, Spokesman For A Middle Class America(Urbana, Ill. 1978)

Connolly, Harold X., A Ghetto Grows in Brooklyn(New York, 1977).

Conyngham, D.P., The Irish Brigade (New York 1867).

Cook, Adrian, The Armies of the Streets, the New York City Draft Riots of 1863(Lexington, Kentucky 1974).

Corbett, Cynthia, Useful Art Long Island Pottery(Setauket, N.Y., 1985).

Costello, Augustine E., Our Police Protectors History of the New York Police, 2 vols., vol. 1(New York, 1885).

Davis, William C., Duel Between the First Ironclads(Garden City, N.Y., 1975).

Dear Brother Walt, edited by Dennis Berthold and Kenneth M. Price, (Kent, Ohio, 1984).

Dolkart, Andrew S., This Is Brooklyn(Brooklyn, 1990).

Donnelly, Ralph W., The Confederate States Marine Corps: The Rebel Leathernecks(Shippensburg, Pa., 1989).

The Diary of George Templeton Strong, edited by Allan Nevins and Milton H. Thomas, 4 vols., Vol. 3(New York, 1952).

Emilio, Luis F., Brave Black Regiment(N.Y., 1894).

Encyclopedia of Historic Forts, edited by Robert B. Roberts(New York, 1988).

Ernst, Robert, <u>Immigrant Life in New York City</u>(Port Washington, N.Y., 1949).

Everdell, William R., and MacKay, Malcolm, <u>Rowboats to Rapid Transit</u> (Brooklyn, 1973).

Freeman, Andrew, <u>Mr. Lincoln Goes to New York</u>(N.Y., 1960).

Gibson, Florence E., <u>The Attitudes of the New York Irish Toward the State and National Affairs 1848-1892</u>(N.Y., 1951).

Goss, Warren Lee, <u>Recollections of a Private</u> (New York,1890).

Greene, Robert Ewell, <u>Black Defenders of America 1775-1973</u> (Chicago, 1974).

Hallock, Judith Lee, <u>Braxton Bragg and Confederate Defeat</u> vol. two(Tuscaloosa, 1991).

Headley, Joel T. <u>The Great Riots of New York 1712-1873</u>(N.Y., 1873).

Heidenreich, Frederick J., <u>Old Days and Old Ways in East New York</u>(Brooklyn, 1948).

Henry, Stuart C., <u>Unvanquished Puritan A Portrait of Lyman Beecher</u>(Grand Rapids, 1973).

<u>Herndon's Lincoln</u>, <u>American Historical Landmarks</u>, edited by David F. Hawke(Indianapolis, 1970).

Hibbin, Paxton, <u>Henry Ward Beecher An American Portrait</u>(N.Y., 1927).

<u>The History of the City of Brooklyn</u>, by Henry R. Stiles, 3 vols.(Brooklyn, 1867-1870).

<u>A History of the City of Brooklyn</u>, edited by Henry W.B. Howard, (Brooklyn, 1893), 2 vol.

Hoehling, A.A., <u>Thunder at Hampton Roads</u>(Englewood Cliffs, N.J., 1976).

Holzman, Robert, <u>Adapt or Perish</u>(Hamden, Ct., 1976).

Holloway, Emory, Whitman(N.Y., 1969).

Hoogenboom, Olive, History of the First Unitarian Church of Brooklyn Heights (Brooklyn, 1987).

Kaplan, Justin, Walt Whitman, A Life(New York, 1980).

Lancaster, Clay, Old Brooklyn Heights(Rutland, Vt., 1961).

Landesman, Alter F., A History of New Lots(Port Washington, N.Y. 1977).

The Life and Writings of Abraham Lincoln, edited by Philip Van Doren Stern, (New York, 1940).

Mack, Edward C., Peter Cooper, Citizen of New York(N.Y., 1949).

Marcot, Roy M., Hiram Berdan(Dallas, 1989).

Martin, Ralph G., Jenny(Englewood Cliffs, N.J., 1969)

Marinacci, Barbara, O Wondrous Singer(Cornwall, N.Y., 1970).

McCaffrey, Lawrence J.,The Irish Diaspora in America (Bloomington, Ind., 1976).

McCullough, David, Brooklyn and How It Got That Way(New York, 1983).

McKay, Ernest, The Civil War and New York City(Syracuse, 1990).

McManus, Edgar J., A History of Negro Slavery in New York (Syracuse, 1966).

McPherson, James M., The Negro's Civil War(New York, 1965).
                                    Battle Cry of Freedom(New York, 1988).

Miller, C. Eugene and Steinlage, Forrest F., Der Turner Soldat (Louisville, Ky., 1988).

Miller, James, Miller's New York As It Is(New York, 1866).

Mines, Samuel, Pfizer, An Informal History(New York, 1978)

Mokin, Arthur, Ironclad(Novato, Ca., 1991).

Neu, Irene D., Erastus Corning, Merchant and Financier (Ithaca,N.Y., 1960).

Nichols, James M., Perry's Saints(Boston, 1886).

Nolan, Dick, Benjamin Franklin Butler, The Damndest Yankee (Novato, Ca., 1991).

Oates, Stephen, With Malice Toward None(New York, 1977)

(O'Connell, J.C., The Irish in the Revolution and the Civil War (Washington, D.C. 1903).

Odell, George C., Annals of the New York Stage, 15 vols., vol. 3 (New York, 1931).

Official Records, War of the Rebellion, Series II, Vol. I, The Maryland Arrests.

Ostrander, Stephen M., A History of the City of Brooklyn, 2 vols., vol. 2.(Brooklyn, 1894).

Palmer, Abraham, History of the 48th Regiment of New York in the War for the Union(Brooklyn, 1885).

Pessen, Edward, Riches, Class and Power Before the Civil War (Lexington, Mass., 1973).

Raymond, Joseph H., The History of Long Island College Hospital and Its Graduates(Brooklyn, 1899).

Rosenwaike, Ira, Population History of New York City(Syracuse 1972)

Scott, John Anthony, The Ballad of America(N.Y., 1966)

Selected Letters From Walt Whitman, edited by Edwin Miller(Iowa City, 1990).

Seymour, Harold, Baseball, The Early Days(New York 1950).

Sharp, Reverend John J., Priests and Parishes of the Diocese of Brooklyn 1820-1944(Brooklyn, 1944).

Shroth, Raymond A., The Eagle and Brooklyn, Westport, Ct., 1974).

Smith, George Winston, Medicines For The Union

Army(Madison, Wisconsin, 1962).

Spalding, Albert G., <u>America's National Game</u>(New York, 1911).

Starfield, Martin J. <u>Highlights of Brooklyn Heights</u>(Brooklyn, 1987)

Starr, Louis M., <u>The Bohemian Brigade</u>(New York, 1954).

Still, William S.,<u>The Commanding Officers of the U.S.S. Monitor</u> (Greenville,N.C. 1988)

Sutherland, Daniel, <u>The Confederate Carpetbaggers</u>(Baton Rouge 1988).

Swanberg, W. A., <u>First Blood</u>(New York, 1957).

<u>Sickles the Incredible</u>(N.Y., 1956)

Syrett, Harold, <u>The City of Brooklyn 1865-1898 A Political History</u>(New York, 1944).

Thomas, Benjamin, <u>Abraham Lincoln A Biography</u>(N.Y., 1952)

Trudeau, Noel, <u>Bloody Roads South</u>(N.Y., 1989)

<u>Walt Whitman's Civil War</u>, edited by Walter Lowenfels, (New York, 1960).

<u>Walt Whitman and the Civil War</u>, edited by Charles I. Glicksberg, (New York, 1933).

<u>Walt Whitman's New York</u>, edited by Henry M. Christman(New York 1963).

Wald, Ralph Forster, <u>Brooklyn is America</u>(New York, 1950)

<u>War of the Rebellion</u>, compiled by Frederick Phisterer, (Albany, 1890).

Weiss, Gustav, <u>The Book of Porcelain</u>(Berlin, 1964), translated by Janet Seligman (N.Y., 1971).

Wheeler, Francis B., <u>The First Monitor and its Builders</u>(Poughkeepsie, 1884).

Whitman, Walt, <u>Leaves of Grass</u>, introduction by Gay Wilson Allen, (New York, 1958).

White, Ruth, <u>Yankee From Sweden</u>(N.Y.,1960).

Wickware, Francis Sill, <u>The House of Squibb</u>(New York, 1965).

Wittke, Carl, <u>We Who Built America</u>(Case Western Reserve University, 1939)

Wolfe, Gerard R., <u>New York, A Guide to the Metropolis</u>(New York, 1975).

Younger, William Lee, <u>Old Brooklyn in Early Photographs</u>(New York, 1978).

Newspapers

New York <u>Times</u>

Brooklyn <u>City News</u>

Brooklyn <u>Standard</u>

Brooklyn <u>Era</u>

Brooklyn <u>Eagle</u>

Brooklyn <u>Daily Union</u>

Brooklyn <u>Evening Star</u>

Brooklyn <u>Daily Times</u>

<u>Drumbeat</u>

Pamphlets and Brochures

Brooklyn Almanac

The Great Divine Henry Ward Beecher

Brujkleen Colonie 1638-1918

Factories, Foundries and Refineries

Brooklyn Old and New

Main Artery

Weeksville Curriculum Unit, Project Weeksville

Weeksville Then and Now

Black Churches in Brooklyn

Brooklyn's Red Legged Devils at Gettysburg

Centennial at St. Patrick's Church, Brooklyn

Cornelius Bushnell

Corning Glass Works Historical Timeline

Beer in the American Home

An Historical and Descriptive Review of the City of Brooklyn

80th Anniversary Year Abraham and Strauss

Growing Up in Brooklyn

Historic and Beautiful Brooklyn

A History of Fort Hamilton and Vicinity 1654-1942

Historic Fort Hamilton

Historic Greenpoint

John Ericsson

Magazine of History Extra edition No. 13, 1911

Monitor

Negro History Bulletin

One Hundredth Anniversary of the R.C. Diocese of Brooklyn 1853-1953

People of Brooklyn

St. John's Semi-centennial, 1834-1884

A Short History of the Naval Yard

Union Temple of Brooklyn 100 year commemmorative

Dissertations and theses

Duduit, James M., <u>Henry Ward Beecher and the Political Pulpit</u>, doctoral dissertation, Florida State University, 1983.

Joyce, William L., <u>Editors and Ethnicity, A History of the Irish-American Press 1848-1883</u>, doctoral dissertation, University of Michigan, 1974.

Karnbach, William F., <u>Two Mayors of Brooklyn During the</u>

Civil War, master's degree thesis, New York University, 1961.

Rosen, Elliot A., The Growth of the American City, 1830-1860, doctoral dissertation, New York University, 1953.

Schoenbaum, Eleonora, Emerging Neighborhoods and the Development of Brooklyn Fringe Areas, 1850-1930, doctoral dissertation, Columbia University, 1977.

Victory, James J., The Promise At The Doorstep, master's degree thesis, St. John's University, 1979.

Articles

America's Gideon in the "Scepter Isle:" The British Tour of Henry Ward Beecher, by Edward W. Ellsworth, Lincoln Herald, 1971.

Black Chaplains in the Union Army, by Edwin G. Redkey, Civil War History, December 1987.

Brooklyn in the Election of 1860, by Donald E. Simon, New-York Historical Society Quarterly, July 1967.

The Great Civil War Hoax, by Jeffrey D. Wert, American History Illustrated, April 1980.

How We Found the Monitor, by John G. Newton, National Geographic, January 1975.

Monitor Companies: A Study of the Major Firms That Built the U.S.S. Monitor, by William H. Still, American Neptune, Spring 1988

New York Ferryboats in the Union Navy, by Rachel Minick, New-York Historical Society Quarterly, January 1965.

The Pieces of a Puzzle, by Robert J. Swan, Weeksville Historical Research Review, 1971.

Political Nativism in Brooklyn, by Richard J. Purcell and John F. Poole, American Irish Historical Society Journal, 1941.

The Revolving Turret and its Inventor, Theodore Timby, by H.H. Guernsey, Harpers Magazine, January 1963.

Slavery on Long Island, A Study of Economic Motivation, by Ralph R. Ireland, Journal of Long Island History, Spring l966.

Some Pre-Civil War Irish Militiamen of Brooklyn, by William Harper Bennett, The American Irish Historical Society Journal, 1922.

The Squibb laboratory in 1863, The Journal of the history of medicine, July 1958.

Miscellaneous

Beecher Family Papers, B.H.S.

Beecher Family Papers, Yale University Library

Havemeyer Family Records, N.Y.H.S.

Letters of Walt Whitman, the Berg Collection, N.Y.P.L.

Manual of the Common Council of the city of Brooklyn, 1863, N.Y.P.L.

Microfiche, Samuel Liebmann, B.H.S.

Murals, Muse Museum

Old Brooklyn Heights 1827-1927, Commemorative, Brooklyn Savings Bank

Rare Account From Aboard the Monitor, from the Civil War Round Table of Buffalo newsletter, January 1992

Report number 144, 47th Congress, 1st session House of Representatives, 1882. B.H.S.

Stillwell Family Papers, 1727-1871, Manuscript Division, N.Y.P.L.

United States Colored Troops Field and Staff Muster Roll, 1863

INDEX